Darlin', you're ogling me like I was the ghost of Elvis come back to check into this little Heartbreak Hotel of yours. I don't suppose you'd want to tell me why that is?"

"I—we..." She fanned her flushed cheeks with an open hand.

"Have we met before?"

Her lips fell open as if to answer 'yes,' but the long waves of her hair moved gently as she shook her head 'no' instead.

Cameron smiled and leaned against the door frame, stealing a moment to study the woman he had sought out. Julia Reed. He'd had her profile and all pertinent information pulled up last night. Just a matter of a phone call and a few computer keystrokes for a veteran agent such as himself. A mish-mash of the collected facts about the woman in question ran through his mind.

Post baby boomer, community do-gooder, regular church goer—though she did miss on occasion when she attended street corner services with the shelter chaplain. She'd chipped a tooth when she was twelve, broken an engagement when she was twenty-one. No subversive affiliations. No suspicious activities. No husband, no kids—not even a dog depended on this woman. Yet, Cameron got the feeling anyone could depend on her.

At least he hoped so, because he needed to depend on her—and before it was all said and done, she would need to depend on him, too.

Palisades.
Pure Romance.

FICTION THAT FEATURES CREDIBLE CHARACTERS AND

ENTERTAINING PLOT LINES, WHILE CONTINUING TO UPHOLD

STRONG CHRISTIAN VALUES. FROM HIGH ADVENTURE

TO TENDER STORIES OF THE HEART, EACH PALISADES

ROMANCE IS AN UNDILUTED STORY OF LOVE,

FROM BEGINNING TO END!

IRISH EYES

ANNIE JONES

PALISADES

IRISH EYES
published by Palisades
a part of the Questar publishing family

© 1997 by Luanne Jones

Published in association with the literary agency of
Writer's House, Inc.

International Standard Book Number: 1-57673-108-1

Cover illustration by JoAnn Weistling
Cover design by Mona Weir-Daly
Edited by Jennifer Brooks

Printed in the United States of America

Scripture quotations are from: *The Revised Standard Version* (RSV)
© 1971 by Zondervan Publishing House

For information:
QUESTAR PUBLISHERS, INC.
POST OFFICE BOX 1720
SISTERS, OREGON 97759

Library of Congress Cataloging-in-Publication Data
Jones, Annie.
Irish eyes/by Annie Jones. p.cm.ISBN 1-57673-108-1 (alk. paper) I. Title
   PS3560.045744173   1997   96-54716
   813'.54—dc21   CIP

97 98 99 00 01 02 03 04 — 10 9 8 7 6 5 4 3 2 1

For Amy McGuffey
and James Dobben

May God bless you on the occasion
of your engagement!

May there always be work for your hands to do.
May your purse always hold a coin or two.
May the sun always shine on your window pane.
May the rainbow be certain to follow the rain.
May the hand of a friend always be near you.
May God fill your heart with gladness to cheer you.

—IRISH BLESSING

Come to me, all who labor and are heavy laden,
and I will give you rest.

MATTHEW 11:28

Prologue

T hose eyes.

Julia Reed blinked. She tried to hunker down to an inconspicuous size in the driver's seat of her rattletrap, mostly blue car. Her heart skipped, making her breath catch in the back of her throat.

Never had she seen such vital, expressive eyes as those in the tanned, rugged face turned toward her.

The sounds of traffic whirred in the background, punctuated by the jarring jangle of bells from the door of the minimarket a few feet away. She scanned the storefront. Cigarette ads, posters of upcoming events, even the latest sale price of soda pop competed for her attention.

None of them could distract her from the sight of the man with the softly curling golden hair, leaning against the pay phone, with a rainbow touching his broad left shoulder.

Play the Lucky Jackpot Lotto! the poster behind him enticed.

His gaze found hers.

She bit her lower lip.

He tucked his hand into the pocket of his faded jeans, pushing up the hem of his creamy Irish-knit sweater. He looked for all the world to her like the very pot of gold at the rainbow's end.

A wordless tune began rambling through her mind.

She pressed her lips together, realizing that she had instinctively parted them to speak to the stranger through her open window.

The passenger door creaked open.

"Let's get cruising. I have a life, you know—and big plans for tonight."

She twisted her head to stare at her assistant, Craig Davis, who had run into the store for her out of sheer impatience. The car dipped as he threw his lanky form into the seat, setting a white plastic bag between them. "Got everything on your grocery list."

He handed her two lonely dollar bills and some change, which she stuffed into her jeans pocket with resignation.

"Since that didn't totally tap out your funds, I got you a treat—a candy bar."

Before she could scold him for the extravagance, he pulled the door shut with a firm clank and said, "Are you okay? You look kind of, um, dazed or something."

"I was just thinking." Her long hair snagged on the tattered upholstery as she twisted her head toward the pay phone to steal another glimpse of the man with the twinkling green eyes and the faint quirk of a smile.

He was gone.

She was just thinking, she finished in silence, that she would have liked to have said something to him, to have seen if his voice matched the compelling image of masculine strength and boyish mischief she saw conveyed in his intense gaze. That's all.

"You were thinking what?" Craig asked.

"Never mind." She sighed.

The Lord worked in mysterious ways. Maybe she would see the man again. She did spend a lot of time in this part of town, after all. She'd keep her eyes open for him. Just to satisfy her curiosity about his voice, she told herself. She'd recognize him at once just by looking into those fabulous eyes.

She cranked the key in the ignition. The car coughed to life, then lurched backwards out of the parking space. She drove off, humming through her involuntary smile the song that had popped into her head.

"When Irish eyes are smilin'..."

W *in the Lucky Jackpot Lottery.* The glittering rainbow arched against the gray Cincinnati sky, stilling the song on Julia's lips. She guided her old clunker of a car into the exit lane so that she would pass directly alongside the glaring billboard promising riches.

Turn one dollar into millions! The golden coins brimming over the lip of a fat black pot on the sign seemed to wink at her, beckoning. The two crisp dollar bills stuffed in her jeans pocket crackled quietly as she shifted in her bottomed-out bucket seat.

Two dollars. The change Craig had returned to her after filling her meager grocery list was all the money she had to get her through until payday. Assuming they could afford to actually pay her at the end of this week.

If only there were a real way to turn her last two dollars into the money she needed to save the homeless shelter she directed. Maybe if she—

Quiet thunder shook the sky.

"This is the voice of your conscience speaking."

Julia blinked, then tossed a quick glance at Craig in the seat next to hers.

He beamed a teasing grin at her, poked his wire-rimmed glasses up onto the bridge of his nose, then placed his curled fingers to his lips like the mouthpiece of a trumpet. "Weee-ooo. Weee-ooo. Temptation alert! Temptation alert! Woman in sector five considering spending her last few dollars on lottery tickets."

"I am not," she snapped, then backpedaled. "Well, not exactly."

"C'mon, Julia, you can't fool me. Whatever goes through your head shines right out those big baby blues of yours, and do you know why?"

"The question should be, 'Do I *want* to know why?' And the answer is 'no.'" She edged her car into the sluggish line of traffic creeping up to the expressway. The sign loomed nearer.

"The reason I can tell exactly what you're thinking before you say a word, my fair Miss Reed," Craig continued, undisturbed by her surly mood, "is because you are a woman completely without guile."

"Goodness!" She opened her eyes wide and her lips circled in mock surprise. "I wish you'd told me this sooner, Craig. If I'd known I was completely without it, I could have picked some up at the market a minute ago."

"Better that than a lottery ticket," he needled.

Julia had to smile at his persistence and good intentions. "I wasn't seriously considering it, just daydreaming. You know, playing 'what if?'"

"You have a better chance of being struck by lightning than winning the lottery," he told her quietly.

The cloudy skies rumbled overhead.

Julia rolled her eyes. "Thanks for sharing, Craig."

"Things will work out for the shelter, Julia, you'll see." He angled his narrow shoulders toward her and settled his frame into the worn seat.

"I wish I had your—" *Faith*. That was the expression, but in this case it didn't fit. Julia had faith. Even through all she'd seen and experienced since coming to work for St. Patrick's Homeless Shelter, she'd never wavered in her trust in God. Faith she had. It was money she lacked, money for her own needs now as well as the shelter's.

"I wish I had your positive outlook," she told her assistant.

The car's engine growled as her foot pressed heavily on the gas pedal. She pulled the steering wheel sharply to the right, following the sloping curve to the expressway. As they pulled parallel to the billboard, she couldn't resist taking one last, wistful peek.

"Would you look at that?" She uttered a low groan, then swerved the car onto the gravel shoulder of the exit ramp, stopping dead even with the huge sign, which was actually two billboards back-to-back.

"What?" Craig squinted from behind his thick lenses.

"That." She pointed to a thin ribbon of smoke spiraling upward between the billboards' twin support posts. Below that, the green-black glimmer of wind-battered garbage bags covered the space between the posts. "It looks like someone is trying to set up housekeeping without a house."

Her cluttered keychain jangled as she turned the car off. The engine sputtered and coughed, then finally slumped into silence. Before Craig could voice a protest, she opened her door and swung her long legs out.

He leaned across the seat as if to snatch her and keep her from getting out of the car. "You can't save them all, Julia."

Her feet hit the ground, and she slipped out of the car. "No, but maybe I can save this one."

She braced herself against the hood of the car, the engine's warmth seeping into her flattened palms. She narrowed her eyes to size up the situation under the billboard.

Satisfied that it was not especially dangerous, she peeked

inside the car again. "It looks pretty typical. Care to join me in extending the hand of welcome?"

Craig set his lips in a thin line and glowered at her.

She held his steady gaze.

Finally, he huffed and rolled his eyes. The passenger door clanked as he popped it open.

"Oh, and bring that bag of groceries, will you? If whoever is under that sign won't go to the shelter, at least we can leave those."

Craig snagged the plastic bag and wrangled it out of the car. "This is your food, Julia," he protested. "If you give it away, what are you going to eat?"

"I'll be fine, Craig." She waved away his very real concern. "It's not like I can't stand to lose a few pounds."

"Maybe you should start by unloading the weight of the world you try to carry on your shoulders."

Julia pretended she didn't hear the mumbled assessment. She tugged at the hem of her shapeless sweater, then stepped lightly up the gentle embankment toward the billboard. Her tattered loafers sank into the muck of the soggy spring ground, the moisture seeping through where the stitches had broken in the sole. She wiggled her chilled toes in her damp socks and tossed back the long tangles of wavy black hair that had fallen over her shoulder.

Her long legs made it easy for her to climb over the broken-down wire fence between the exit ramp and the billboard.

Craig kept at her heels, his unhappiness evident in the heavy sighs that reached her ears every few moments.

The chances were that she was about to try to help someone who would be as thrilled with her offer as her assistant was to tag along behind her. Julia trudged on. Even if this unseen person did accept the warmth and safety of the shelter for the night, that was not a long-range solution.

And as temporary solutions went, Julia thought glumly as she scaled the hillside, her foundering shelter seemed more temporary than most. Unless something changed very soon, St. Patrick's would shut down in six short weeks.

Still, it would provide a hot meal and dry place to sleep tonight—and that beat camping out under a billboard.

"Excuse me," she called out. "I don't mean you any trouble, but I noticed your campsite."

No answer.

She glanced at Craig.

He shrugged and cast a longing look back at the car waiting for them.

"Um, I'm the director of St. Patrick's Homeless Shelter and this is my assistant. We just wanted to let you know we can find you a place to sleep tonight, if you'd like."

"Be off with you."

Julia started at the distinct Irish brogue in the voice coming from beneath the billboard. Was her fascination with the man at the pay phone making her hear things? The firm tone held no hint of threat, just an obvious desire to be left alone, so she decided to press the matter a bit.

"Look, I'm not going to drag you out of there or anything. If you're an adult, capable of making your own decisions about where you spend the night, it's not my place to force you into a shelter," she said in a soothing, yet no-nonsense voice.

The wind whipped her hair across her face and she tossed her head to clear her view. "But it looks like a real storm brewing tonight, and I just wanted you to know there's a warm bed and hot meal available if you want to get out of the elements for a night."

"I do no' wish it," the voice barked. "And I don't wish to be having any callers. Now, away with you."

Once she overcame her shock at the accent, something else

about the voice disturbed her. She couldn't decide what, though. As she tried to pinpoint her misgivings, she realized she couldn't even tell if it was a man or woman speaking. The building howl of the wind and steady whooshing of passing cars didn't help.

She squinted into the dimming light of the approaching evening and concentrated, hoping the voice would speak again. When it didn't she felt she had no choice but to do what she could and go on.

"At least let me leave these groceries for you."

She stretched her arm out to Craig to take the bag filled with the staples she'd hoped would get her through the week.

"Groceries?" Even through the thick accent, suspicion colored the word.

Julia glanced at Craig and gave a confident nod. She'd piqued the person's interest.

"It isn't much." She lifted the bag up. The white plastic rustled in the swirling wind. "Just a few things I picked up on my way home from work."

"You'd give me the food meant for your own table?" The hushed question in the sweet, lilting brogue seemed to carry on the wind to her.

Julia smiled. She'd made a connection.

She lifted the bag higher. "I only wish it could be more."

"'Tis a trick."

"No, really, it isn't."

Her top teeth scraped across her lower lip and she gave Craig an anxious look.

He shook his head.

Not this one, Julia, he seemed to be saying.

She sighed. Even after all these years, it tugged at her heart not to be able to reach someone. But Craig was right. The storm could break out at any moment and they couldn't stay any longer. She could only leave the groceries and hope that tomorrow her outreach workers could coax the person in.

"We're going now," she told the voice. She set the bag down in the thick grass at her feet and stepped back. "Why don't you come get these before they get rained on?"

"How do I know you won't snatch me once I come out? Or, for that matter, that what you've got in that wee bag is worth the leaving of me humble abode?"

"Humble abode?" Craig whispered. "Who's he kidding? If that abode were any humbler it would be a hole in the ground."

"Regardless of that fact, Craig," she said, smiling at the charm of the phrase in this situation, "this is a fellow human being and we must be—"

"Out of our ever-lovin' minds," he teased, flipping the collar of his jacket up against a sudden gust. He directed his gaze toward the flapping garbage bags. "Look here, pal, it's nothing fancy, but it's what the lady planned to live on for a few days. Some bread and peanut butter—"

"And jelly?" the voice asked.

"Sorry, no jelly." Julia said, craning her neck to see if she could spot the speaker. "But there are three apples and a candy bar, and half a gallon of milk."

"Milk? Did you say milk?"

The mysterious loner had been hooked.

She stepped back to show she meant no aggression and said, "Half a gallon of cold, sweet milk."

"All right, then. Leave the bag and be on your way."

"I'm going." She took another backward step, sensing more than seeing that Craig had done the same.

"At least now we know he won't go hungry," she whispered to her assistant from the side of her mouth.

"Yeah, but you will." Craig turned to hurry on down the hill to the car.

21

Julia followed suit, but she couldn't resist a quick glimpse over her shoulder.

"No." Her open hand made a dull thud as she clapped it to her chest.

No matter how many times she encountered it in her line of work, each time she came across a child living in the streets—or in this case, beside the expressway—it had a profound, chilling effect upon her.

No way would she let this little redheaded imp slip back under that billboard to spend another night on his own. Luckily for her, the boy, clad in a green windbreaker and surprisingly clean jeans, had stopped to rifle through the contents of the bag. Withdrawing the milk, the boy ripped open the half-gallon carton and began swigging down its contents.

Julia shifted her weight toward the boy.

Craig leaned toward her, placing his hand on her arm.

She flinched, ready to pull free if he tried to stop her from intervening in this situation.

"Go for it, Julia," he whispered. "You get the kid. I'll be ready if he makes a break for it."

"Thanks." She patted his hand.

Three strides brought her almost on top of the child, who didn't seem to notice her until she wrapped her arms around his waist. "Gotcha."

"You said you wouldn't be snatching me," the child roared as he thrashed from side to side in her grasp.

"I said no such thing." She tightened her hold, tipping her head up to keep the churning headful of red curls from crashing into her chin.

"You said you had no right to be forcing me into your shelter," he reminded her as droplets of milk from the open carton splashed in her face.

"I said I couldn't force you if you were an adult—but you're not." She thanked Craig with a nod when he strode up to take the carton. "There is no way I'm going to leave you out here alone."

"Do you have any idea the kind of danger a kid like you is in on your own?" Craig asked.

"I'm not—"

"Not what?" Julia demanded. "You're not going to try to tell me you're not a kid, are you?"

The boy's emerald green eyes flashed in panic as he shifted his gaze to Craig, then Julia, then to their surroundings. He hunched his slender shoulders.

"Th-that's right, lass, that's just what I'll be telling you." The lie was neither well-planned nor well-presented. He ducked his head and could not keep his gaze fixed to hers.

Julia couldn't help but wonder what he had been going to say—that he was not alone? Could he be protecting someone? She scanned the area but could not see anyone else in or near the makeshift campsite.

As if he sensed her suspicions, the boy raised his shoulders and cocked his head, his voice wavering but loud. "I'm telling you I'm no more a kid than you are."

To emphasize this point he swung his legs back, trying to kick her shins.

She set his feet soundly on the ground and leaned in to speak clearly in his ear. "Here's a helpful hint: next time you try to convince someone of your maturity, leave off the part where you throw a temper tantrum."

Craig took one of the boy's arms and she the other. He sulked along between them all the way to the car.

"Listen, son, don't feel bad that you got caught. I'm an old hand at this kind of thing," Julia told him, trying to keep the lines of communication open. "I've been a social worker for over a decade. Six years in the Department of Child Welfare and the last four running a homeless shelter."

She helped him over the fence, keeping a firm but gentle grip on the scruff of his neck. Her feet were nearly frozen now, and to add insult to inconvenience, her struggle with the boy had caused milk to spill down her leg and drip into one sorry excuse for a shoe.

Her discomfort probably fueled her weary sarcasm as she prodded him toward her car. "There isn't a story you can concoct that I haven't heard, son—and in several languages, to boot. Nothing you can say will make me leave a child to spend a single night on the streets alone."

"But I tell you, I am no child," the boy insisted.

"Let me guess," Craig strode forward and opened the back door of the car. "If you're not a kid, judging from that accent, flaming red hair and green jacket, it's obvious to anyone with eyes—you're a leprechaun."

The boy, whose movements had already stilled, went positively rigid. The flash in his green eyes quieted, and he tipped his chin up at a proud angle. "I am."

"You are what?" Craig crowned the bright red curls with his large palm to try to urge the boy inside the car.

The boy jerked his head away. "I am one of the little people of Ireland—a leprechaun."

A stress-breaking bubble of laughter burst from Julia's lips. As lies went, this one was a whopper. But it was original, she had to give the boy that. He had to be protecting something—or someone—pretty important to try anything this creative to distract them.

"Well, I have to admit, you've got me there, kiddo. That is one story I've never heard," she said. "But just because you're a terrific storyteller doesn't change the fact that you're a minor in need of assistance."

"I'm no miner." A resigned grin broke across his face, his

green eyes glinting in mischief. "Leprechauns don't mine their gold, they bury it. You must be thinking of dwarfs."

"No, I'm thinking of dinner, and how standing here listening to your nonsense is keeping me from it." Craig set Julia's groceries inside the car and motioned for the boy to get in as well.

"I don't suppose you want to tell us your name?" Julia asked through the open driver's door as the boy curled up in the back seat and Craig plunked down in the passenger's side.

"Oh, no, you won't be tricking that out of me." He scowled up at her.

"Why not? Is that some kind of leprechaun superstition?" She regretted the bitter tinge of her words, but she was cold and tired. Tired, not just from the grueling day-after-day struggle for the shelter's survival, but tired to the depths of her spirit over situations just like this one. It sometimes seemed that every day, more and more hands stretched out in need, and fewer and fewer reached back, ready to help.

Craig slammed his door shut. "Whatever we're going to do, Julia, could we get on with it?"

She sighed and folded her hands on top of the car, scanning the thinning traffic in the dim evening light. Darkness and stormy weather were fast approaching, her car was on a ramp headed away from any facilities that could take this child for the night, and Craig had made it clear he had plans and would not welcome delay.

A passing car flicked on its headlights. Thunder resonated from deep inside the billowing gray clouds. If only she could find a police car and wave it over—that would be ideal.

"I'll tell you what, my little lucky charmer, I could use some leprechaun magic right now," she muttered, even as she bowed her head to utter a brief prayer for guidance and whatever help might come her way.

"What is it you'd wish for, lass?" The child's slight weight moved the old car as he leaned forward to peer up at her from behind the driver's seat.

What is it you'd wish for? The question echoed through her being. She knew what she must pray for, what she must work for, even what she would hope for, but what would she wish for? The distinction of the single word gave her a wistful feeling, like a child with her pencil poised over a Christmas list.

"Days like this, my friend, which for me are pretty much every day, I think I'd wish—" She imagined enough money to afford a hot meal out somewhere, nothing fancy but filling; decent shoes; and the shelter full of volunteers, its bankrolls filled to capacity, its occupancy at an all-time low. She sighed. "I guess I'd just wish—for a little help."

"Granted." The word rushed out like a breath of fresh Irish breeze.

Julia stared down at the boy, who pressed his lips together the way a child does before he imparts his deepest secret. But before he could utter a single sound, the whoop of a police siren made her jump.

Whirls of red light spun across the scene as an unmarked cruiser pulled up behind her old car.

A wave of relief washed over her, sweeping away the dim cast of her mood. She glanced from the stopping police car to the boy and grinned. "I suppose you're going to try to claim this is all courtesy of your benevolent blarney, Mr. Leprechaun."

"No need to thank me, lass. I'll just be on my way."

"Oh, no, you don't." Craig lurched after the boy, but the youngster was too fast. He slipped away and out the car door.

"Hold it right there." Julia fell into her I'll-brook-no-argument-from-you voice with great ease. She snagged the boy, who glanced toward the cruiser and the officer climbing out of it with anxiety in his green eyes.

"I'm telling you," the boy said in a harsh whisper, "I'm a leprechaun. I've granted your wish for help, now you have to let me go."

He fought like a wildcat for release, but Julia held firm.

"Stop that this instant," she said, then let her tone soften to show the real empathy she felt for the child. "Listen, sweetie, I know a kid in your situation has a natural distrust of the police, but I promise you, the officer is here to help you. This is really for the best. We can't leave you out here alone."

"I'm not..." he clamped his mouth shut.

Alone. He didn't have to say it for Julia to hear it. She glanced to the billboard but saw no other sign of life there.

She returned her gaze to meet the boy's, searching for the answers he masked with a flash of defiance.

Beyond them, she heard the swish of the policeman's boots in the tall roadside grass. Craig slammed his car door and came around to stand beside her.

"Are you waiting for someone special?" she asked the boy.

That struck a chord in her young companion. He started, but still kept his lips sealed in a grim line.

"What? Do you think there are other leprechauns lurking about, Julia?" Craig teased, his own mood obviously lightened now that it was clear this mess wouldn't completely ruin his plans for the night. "Why bother with those? You've already caught your limit, and besides that, he hasn't forked over his pot of gold."

The boy went rigid beneath her restraining hand.

"Don't be silly, Craig," she said, trying to keep everyone calm until the policeman, who was scribbling down her license plate number, got to them.

"It's not silly, Julia," Craig protested, poking his glasses back on the bridge of his nose. He sniffled in the damp air. "The legend goes, if you catch a leprechaun, he has to surrender his pot of gold. Isn't that right, Red?"

The boy's green eyes sparked. "Indeed it is. Now, if you'll excuse me, I'll just be getting that gold..."

Julia tightened her grip and added a small shake, which was really meant for her assistant. "Don't go putting ideas in his head, Craig."

"What seems to be the problem here, ma'am?" The tall, imposing officer strolled up to their little tableau, his face partially obscured by the brim of his dark brown hat.

"Hello, sir. I'm Julia Reed, director of St. Patrick's Homeless Shelter." She extended her right hand. "I am so glad you came along when you did, Officer...?"

"Shaughnessy." He took her hand and gave it one jerking shake. "Michael Shaughnessy."

Was it her imagination, Julia wondered, or did the man's presence make the child bristle more than it should?

"How can I help you?" Officer Shaughnessy asked, his gaze fixed on the boy.

The gesture made Julia shiver, but she fought off any apprehensions by concluding that perhaps the two had had run-ins before. Street kids and cops did not mix well, at any rate, so even if there was nothing personal between the two, they would respond as adversaries out of habit.

"Um, you can't help me, exactly, Officer," Julia said, caution coloring her words. "It's this fellow here."

She moved to ruffle the boy's hair, but he dodged the overture.

"We found the kid trying to take up residence—without a residence." Craig folded his arms over his narrow chest and hiccuped a kind of laugh at his word play.

"I see," the officer said, his voice flat. "Well, you just leave him to me. I'll make sure he's taken care of."

The boy glowered at the uniformed man.

The situation didn't feel right to Julia, but she had no reason for her misgivings. Swallowing down the cold lump in her throat, she reached in her back jeans pocket to find a business card.

"If you need anything, son, please call." She offered the card to the boy. "Here's how you can find me."

He turned his angry eyes to her and kept his arms at his sides.

Julia cast her gaze to the soggy ground. She set her jaw and tucked the card in her front pocket, letting it poke out so she could whip it free if she sensed a change in the boy's attitude.

The police officer stepped up. His huge hand grasped the boy by the jacket collar, throwing the child off balance for a moment.

Suddenly, the boy shot away from the officer, straight into Julia.

The force of the boy's weight made her stagger backward a few steps, but she quickly regained her footing. The boy moved around so he was standing half behind her, and she automatically straightened up in a defensive posture.

The officer tensed and she wondered if she—or the boy— was in danger.

"Please, lass, please." The pure pleading nature of the boy's voice tugged at her heart, and she turned her head to meet his desperate gaze.

"Leave the boy to me, ma'am," Officer Shaughnessy barked.

"One moment," she responded, making it clear she wouldn't allow any quibbling. She focused on the child, who was standing so close she could feel his rabbit-paced heartbeat at her side.

Julia placed one hand on the boy's shoulder. She tried to smile, to offer some gesture of understanding, but the expression on the boy's face told her he was beyond seeing anything

29

but his own goal. She kept her voice low to preclude Craig and the police officer from hearing. "What is it? Don't be afraid, you can tell me."

He did not trust her, that much was clear from his wary stance and nervous fidgeting. The green eyes shifted toward the rainbow-covered billboard and a brightness seemed to pass over his features.

"By rights, my pot o' gold is yours, lass." The lilting words barely carried to her above the din of traffic and the grumble from the skies above. "I can't have it fallin' into another's hands."

Officer Shaughnessy tapped the toe of his boot against a stone jutting from the wet grass. "Hurry it up, will ya?"

The boy's throat tightened with a deep gulp. "Please, lass, you've got to be the one to claim me treasure. Can I have your promise on that?"

She looked steadily into the boy's face, her heart as heavy as the laden rain clouds hanging low over the skyline. The child had no home and few possessions, she realized. The last thing he wanted was to lose the belongings he had managed to squirrel away, those things which he counted as precious as gold—his treasures. And he was asking her for help.

"Julia to the rescue again," she mumbled, her eyes rolling heavenward.

"What was that, lass?"

"I said, sure, I'll look after your treasure." She sighed. "Just tell me where to find it."

"Now, where are you supposin' you'd be finding a pot o' gold, lass?" He wriggled his dark red eyebrows, his glance flicking toward the Lucky Lottery Jackpot Billboard. Their voices blended in a hushed conspiracy. "Under the rainbow."

Julia laughed and shook back her long hair.

"Just find the patch of shamrocks and dig straight down," the boy whispered.

"Dig? I have to dig?"

"Shh!" The boy raised a finger to his lips. "Of course you have to dig for the treasure. Don't you know anything?"

She smoothed her hand over his thick curls and shifted her weight uneasily. "Actually, I'm beginning to think I don't know anything at all."

Lightning ripped across the gray clouds, throwing over the boy's anxious features a mixture of yellow light and shadow.

"If you don't hurry this along, ma'am, we're going to be standing in a rain storm." Officer Shaughnessy shuffled a step closer to them.

"Cuff 'im, book 'im, whatever it takes, Officer," Craig boomed, checking the watch on his bony wrist.

"I'll be coming along with you...sir." The boy turned and walked away from Julia, his shoulders hunched, his feet kicking at the grass as he went.

As the patrol car drove away, Craig clapped his hands together. "Another good deed done in record time. Now if we could just—"

"Not yet." Julia moved to the back of her car to unlock the trunk.

"What are you doing?"

The trunk lid rose to reveal the emergency aid unit she carried with her everywhere.

"If you're doing what I think you're doing," Craig warned her, "you better realize I'm not going to be a party to it. I have—"

She cut him off, turning to rifle through the piles of blankets and extra clothes, spare batteries, flashlights, and first aid kits to produce a sorry excuse for a shovel. She thrust the splintered handle into Craig's hand. "Here you go."

"What's this?" He glared at the rust-covered tool.

"Faith can move mountains, but sometimes it has to do it

one shovelful of dirt at a time. And somebody has to hold that shovel." Julia trudged back up toward the billboard, motioning for her assistant to follow. "That shovel, my friend, is an instrument of faith in action."

"Pardon me if I point out it's also used to dig graves." Craig hoisted it onto his shoulder and slunk along behind her.

Julia chuckled under her breath. She drew in the smell of the impending storm and let it refresh her. "Don't worry, Craig. This won't take long."

"*What* won't take long? Whatever it is, I hope it doesn't involve any smiting of enemies. Because I've read my job description and it definitely does not include smiting."

"I promise, no smiting. We'll only be a few minutes."

"Julia, what is it we—and by that I mean me, with my awesome set of buffed muscles—are going to do with this mighty shovel of faith?"

"Haven't you guessed?" She glanced over her shoulder, smiled, and raised her eyebrow at his almost good-natured sulking. "We're going to do a little mountain moving."

∼ 2 ∼

Gold! Julia shuddered, her hands fisted on the top of her scarred army surplus desk. She stole a sidelong glance at the ominous cadet-blue safe, glinting at her through the half-open closet door in her office on the second floor of the shelter.

Last night she and Craig had gone beneath the billboard expecting to unearth a cache of sports cards, a ball cap, perhaps a piece of jewelry, some memento a boy might call treasure. Instead they'd found gold. Honest-to-goodness, heavy, gleaming handfuls of very old gold coins.

She pushed one long black coil of hair off her shoulder and tugged her red cardigan closed over her white cotton T-shirt. Her shoulders tensed and she felt acid roil in the pit of her stomach. That pot of gold equaled a peck of trouble.

She'd prayed for guidance on the spot, then hauled the find out of the damp, dark ground. She could still smell the fresh dirt clinging like chocolate cake crumbs to the cast iron kettle and lid. Since she'd received no divine message telling her how to proceed, she'd done what she had thought best, what she felt she had to do.

Craig had wanted to stay with her when she informed the police of their discovery, but she hadn't seen the sense of making him miss out on his dinner plans. He'd reluctantly gotten out of the car when she'd stopped at his apartment, after she reassured him that she would head directly back to the shelter. They both felt that was the place to go. With the protectiveness of her staff around her and the gold tucked inside the shelter safe, she could calmly wait for the police to arrive.

That's what she'd intended to do. But this morning she sat in her office at the shelter with the uncomfortable knowledge that she had a fortune in gold sitting just a few feet away.

"Well? What did the police say? Were the coins reported stolen? Is there a reward?" Craig slipped into her office as silently as his squeaking hightop tennis shoes would allow.

"I don't know," she said softly.

"You don't know what?" Craig slid into the broken wingback chair beside her desk. He blinked at her from behind his rounded glasses, his elbows and knees poking out at sharp angles from the swayed seat. "About the reward or if the stuff was stolen?"

"I don't know," she said with more conviction, almost snapping at her assistant. She looked toward the open office door, then cast her gaze around the room, finally coming back to Craig's expectant expression. She wet her lips. "I don't know about the police."

"The—" His brows clashed above his eyes. "Julia, what are you talking about?"

She glanced at the door again and the empty hallway beyond. They were alone. The night staff and evening's residents had gone already. The shelter stood, wrapped in eerie quiet, locked tight until evening. She drummed her fingertips against the scratched paint on her metal desktop and bit her lower lip.

"I'm talking about Officer Shaughnessy," she said finally.

"Officer who?"

"Shaughnessy. The officer who just happened along at the exact time we needed him to spirit away the Irish boy we found."

"Ah, the leprechaun patrol." Craig nodded his head and chuckled.

"You wouldn't be laughing if you knew what I do." She skimmed her finger over the page of scribblings she'd made the night before. "There is no Officer Michael Shaughnessy with the Cincinnati police."

"Maybe he's with the—"

She traced her fingertip downward on her notes. "He's not with the highway patrol, the sheriff's department, or any of the local campus security forces." Her wooden chair creaked as she leaned back in resignation. "Craig, he's not even a mall cop."

"You're kidding."

She shook her head. "I checked everywhere. Michael Shaughnessy is a great big fake."

Craig's pale skin went almost pure white. "And we turned that kid over to him."

"That kid—who told us where to dig up a fortune," she added.

He hunched his shoulders forward. "What now?"

"I don't know, but—" She checked out the doorway one more time, then inched close to her desk, lowering her upper body and her voice. "I've still got the gold."

"What?" He nearly leaped out of his chair.

"Shh." She placed her finger to her lips. "Think about it, Craig, a boy who knew the whereabouts of something so valuable, kidnapped by a man sneaky enough to impersonate a police officer? If I had turned that gold over to the police, it might have been like signing that child's death warrant."

"And since you didn't, it might be like signing your own."

A solid chunk of ice seemed to settle in her throat. She could hardly breathe, let alone swallow. Craig was right, but then, so was she. Her mind raced but no single thought took center stage.

She wanted to go stumbling out to her car and drive away as fast as she could for parts unknown. At the same time, she wanted to stay right there and never leave the relative safety of her familiar surroundings again. For the first time in a long, long time, Julia Reed, mountain mover, had to admit she needed something more than faith and a shovel—she needed help.

"I was going to say top o' the mornin' to you, but as I get a good long look at this place, I'm more in mind of bottom o' the barrel. Looks like I got here just in time."

Irish. The accent, though faint, dripped like melting butter over every syllable from the deep, masculine voice. It sent a tingle through Julia's body and a shiver down her spine. Holding her breath, she snatched a glance at the safe, at Craig's wary gaze, then finally at the source of the pointed remark.

"You." The word whooshed out with the rush of air from her lungs.

Cameron O'Dea made a show of glancing behind himself. His brushed flannel parka rustled, its open zipper cold against his wrist as he flattened his palm to his nubby gray sweater. He cocked his head at the woman with enormous blue eyes who was gaping at him. "Me?"

"You're...oh, my goodness," she whispered.

He raised an eyebrow at her unexpected reaction, then glanced at the young man glaring at him from a poorly patched wingback chair. "I've been known to have this effect on women." Cameron winked at the woman's overt scrutiny. "Not to worry, though. It tends to wear off once they become adjusted to my sparkling personality."

The man harrumphed his opinion of Cameron's jest.

"Darlin', you're ogling me like I was the ghost of Elvis come back to check into this little Heartbreak Hotel of yours. I don't suppose you'd want to tell me why that is?"

"I—we…" She fanned her flushed cheeks with an open hand.

"Have we met before?"

Her lips fell open as if to answer 'yes,' but the long waves of her hair moved gently as she shook her head 'no' instead.

Cameron smiled and leaned against the door frame, stealing a moment to study the woman he had sought out. Julia Reed. He'd had her profile and all pertinent information pulled up last night. Just a matter of a phone call and a few computer keystrokes for a veteran agent such as himself. A mish-mash of the collected facts about the woman in question ran through his mind.

Post baby boomer, community do-gooder, regular church goer—though she did miss on occasion when she attended street corner services with the shelter chaplain. She'd chipped a tooth when she was twelve, broken an engagement when she was twenty-one. No subversive affiliations. No suspicious activities. No husband, no kids—not even a dog depended on this woman. Yet, Cameron got the feeling anyone could depend on her.

At least he hoped so, because he needed to depend on her—and before it was all said and done, she would need to depend on him, too.

He stroked his chin and narrowed one eye as he took in a quick physical survey of her. The blurred picture from a five-year-old newspaper clipping certainly did not do her justice.

A tall woman, he concluded, as a trained professional sizing up a potential suspect. She had a lean build, jet-black hair, and a classic facial structure. He raised his knuckle to his lips, trying not to laugh at the stiff description that sounded like it belonged on a police report. Julia Reed would not be so easily summarized.

Yes, she was tall and there seemed not an ounce of fat on her frame, but there was a fragility about her all the same. No husky Amazon here, but a willowy quality, strong yet flexible.

Her long hair tumbled about her stalwart shoulders like waves over a rocky shore. The flickering overhead light shone across the inky blackness of her curls. Such hair, he decided, would go silver with age. Not gray or white, but silver—noble, dignified silver.

This is the kind of woman a man could grow old with, Cameron thought.

For an instant he felt a twinge of longing for all that he could never have, all that he had vowed he would forgo until he cleared his family name. He couldn't ask any woman to share the taint of the secret he hid. And yet, he had often wished that he could find a woman—perhaps a woman like Miss Julia Reed—and finally make a home.

Funny that only a moment in the presence of this woman should reawaken those old dreams in him. He looked into the depths of those quiet blue eyes, and his heart skipped a hard, unsteady rhythm.

Where had he seen that face before? he wondered. In a dream? No. For too many years he had seen only one thing in his dreams: his goal, his quest, the one reason he got up in the morning and performed a job that no longer held pleasure or promise for him. Except the promise that he might someday accomplish what he had sworn to do long ago—to right an old wrong and wipe away the shame that had covered his family name for three generations. That's why he had come today.

"Who are you and what are you doing here?"

Cameron tore his gaze from the woman and blinked at the

spindly-legged young man who had suddenly bolted up between them.

He pushed off from the door frame with his forearm and stepped inside the room, which looked more like a storage shed for a thrift shop than an office. "I've come to volunteer."

From the corner of his eye he saw Julia stiffen in her seat.

The young man's knobby shoulders slanted back as he bristled in silent challenge.

"And I've come to see Miss Julia Reed." Cameron blasted his would-be nemesis with a smile of practiced affability. "I take it you're not her."

"I'm Julia Reed." She stood.

Good, Cameron thought. *She's the straightforward type.* He'd known she would be, and yet he could not be sure of her. He had every reason to believe that this blue-eyed woman with the spotless record had just last night uncovered enough gold to turn anyone's head—and she may well have kept it.

"Hello, Miss Reed. Cameron O'Dea." He offered his hand freely and withheld his judgment.

She moved past the wary-eyed young man, reaching out in response. Her cool hand pressed inside his warm palm, the effect sending a subtle shockwave straight to his belly. Her long, delicate fingers folded around his and her grip tightened. She met his gaze, unafraid, all pretense aside.

He smiled. He couldn't help himself. Something about the woman brought out the Irish in him. It felt good. Better than he had felt in many a year.

"How do you do, Mr. Cameron O'Dea?"

The sound of his name on her lips sank into his being like the first drops of a soft rain on a desert.

"You say you've come here to volunteer?"

"I spoke with your staff last night, and they had me fill out some forms and told me to report back to you this morning."

Without lying, he'd given her an answer she would accept.

"Did you?" She cocked her head as though considering his claim. "And tell me, Mr. O'Dea, how is it you chose to give your time to St. Patrick's?"

"'Tis an obvious question, isn't it, lass?" he asked, always opting to evade a direct question than to concoct a story.

"Lass?" She cast a shaded glance at the young man at her side, who returned her look with a guarded frown. She cleared her throat and focused on Cameron again. "And just how is it you heard of our shelter?"

Cameron reached into his back pocket and tugged free the small business card he had found half-buried in the loose dirt near the pilfered pot of gold. Earthy smudges darkened the once stark white paper. He hadn't bothered to clean away the evidence of where he had come upon the card, knowing her reaction to it as it was would speak volumes.

With keen-eyed precision, he extended the card toward her.

Her gaze dipped.

Her assistant's rubber-soled shoes squawked on the tile floor as he pivoted to see for himself.

Julia froze, her face ghostly white.

Gotcha. Cameron's smile tugged into a smirk. "Is something wrong, Miss Reed?"

"I...um, no." She stepped backward.

Cameron could see her thought process on her honest, open face. Surprise turned to fear, then to confusion, then to rationalization, and finally cautious relief.

She shook her head, as if to release the last of her negative thoughts, and moved toward her desk. "For a minute, I thought—well, it doesn't matter. You say you filled out one of our volunteer forms?"

She'd find the information she needed there, Julia told her-self. The sheer coincidence of this man, the man she'd seen

40

moments before she found the boy, a man with the same green eyes and traces of the same accent, showing up on the heels of her finding that gold rattled her to her core. The dirty card, which could easily have fallen from her jeans pocket last night, clinched her suspicions.

But what did he want? Why go through the charade of volunteering at the shelter? Julia felt sure the answers lay in that application and a few quick calls to his references—a strict prerequisite to accepting any volunteer.

"I answered every question in excruciating detail," he told her, returning the card to his pocket. "Marital status—single, if it matters—general health, proof of American citizenship. Only in this country would a fellow have to submit himself to everything but a CAT scan to determine his intentions in offering a helping hand."

She smiled at the obvious diversionary humor. But she wasn't so easily distracted. "Have you been in America long, Mr. O'Dea?"

"Long enough to learn the language," he said, a twinkle in his green eyes.

"Oh?" She gripped the cold metal handle of her desk drawer. "What is your native tongue?"

"Blarney," Craig grumbled.

"What?" The drawer grated as she yanked it open. Her gaze flashed from Craig's dour expression to Cameron's brash grin and sparkling eyes. "Oh, of course, English is your native tongue. What was I thinking?"

She wasn't thinking, she told herself. And that could be a dangerous, if not deadly mistake. She pulled a stack of papers from her desk drawer. "Gee, your form is here."

"You thought otherwise?"

She looked up from the small, square letters of Cameron's handwriting to meet his teasing gaze. "Sometimes things get…misplaced around here."

"I can imagine it," he said softly. "In a place as big as this one I assume all manner of things might be lost—and then found again."

He knows about the gold. Her pulse thudded like a death knell in her ears. She wet her parched lips.

"What is it you want, Mr. O'Dea?" She shoved back the hair that had fallen into her face with a trembling hand. "I mean, what do you want to do…here at the shelter?"

"Ah, what is it I do best, is that what you're asking?"

She couldn't stop herself from nodding.

"Well, let's see then." He tapped his finger to his chin and turned his gaze upward. "I'm a dream weaver by trade—a teller of tales, a seeker of knowledge, a practitioner of the occasional sleight of hand."

"Dream weavers we have by the hundreds, my friend," she warned with a smile. Despite her anxiety, she was charmed by his brogue and bravado. "What else have you got for me?"

"Just myself, lass. Nothing more than Cameron O'Dea, part bloodhound, part workhorse, all yours."

Hers. Cameron's volunteer application crinkled in Julia's suddenly damp hand. "That's a generous offer, Mr. O'Dea, but one I may have to decline. If you had some special skill or training that could be used in the shelter…"

"My head may not be filled with the stuff of college degrees and the like, Miss Reed, but it stays pretty cool in an emergency. That's a skill I'd wager you could use."

She swallowed hard.

"I may not have the calluses of a skilled laborer, but these hands are capable of a bit of hard work or of reaching out to someone who needs them."

She glanced down at his open palms. He had good hands, strong and large, with long, blunt fingers and short, clean nails.

He wore no wedding ring, no jewelry of any kind—no hint of who he might be or what he might want.

Julia smoothed her own hand down the leg of her jeans. A thousand shimmering thoughts and emotions swirled through her. Was this man the answer to a prayer or a walking threat to her life?

She raised the volunteer form. "While we can use all the help we can get around here, there are a few things we have to confirm before we can approve your application. We'll call you when—"

"I can wait." He folded his arms over his chest.

She twisted her head to stare at Craig. Normally, she wouldn't put up with this from a potential volunteer, but they both knew this was not a normal situation. She had the feeling that no matter what she did or said, Cameron O'Dea would stand firm.

"Here, give me those, Julia." With two squeaking footsteps, Craig stood next to her. "I'll start checking his references." Craig took the paper and narrowed his eyes into slits behind his wire-framed glasses. "Immediately."

Torn between feeling grateful for her assistant's efficiency and fearful of finding herself alone with the mysterious Cameron O'Dea—and the gold—she nabbed Craig by the arm.

"Here, use the phone in my office," she said, her throat dry. "While you do that I can show Mr. O'Dea around the shelter."

"An excellent suggestion, Miss Reed," Cameron said in a lilting tone. "It'll give you and me some time to get to know one another. After all, I have the feeling we're going to be spending quite a bit of time together."

～ 3 ～

Cameron started to shrug off his parka. Tiny sparks of static electricity popped against the yarn of his sweater. "Mind if I leave this here while I take the tour?"

Yes, she did mind. Very much. She didn't want to give him any reason to return to her office—and the place where the gold was stored—again. Her plan, if anyone could call a few hasty thoughts of a very muddled and worried mind a plan, was to give the man a quick look around the building, conveniently ending at the front door. Then bye-bye, busybody.

Julia whisked her hand over her forehead. "Um, to tell the truth, Mr. O'Dea—"

"And you always tell the truth, I'm sure, Miss Reed."

His benign smile nagged at Julia's conscience. She hadn't lied to anyone—and yet, she didn't feel completely right about her actions. He realized she had something to hide; that much was obvious. She wound her arms around her cardigan, as if folding herself inside a security blanket.

"I do always tell the truth, Mr. O'Dea." She shook her head and felt her hair ruffle over her stiffened spine. "But I don't feel

I have to reveal everything to everyone who walks through my door. Now, if you feel I haven't been truthful with you, perhaps you'd be more comfortable volunteering elsewhere."

He said nothing. Just smiled that heart-tweaking Irish grin of his, those green eyes all but dancing with delight at her display of bravado.

"If you still want that tour, however, I suggest you keep your coat with you." She used one hand to indicate that he should step into the hallway. "We couldn't begin to afford to heat the whole building, and it can get pretty damp and chilly in the basement."

He draped the green parka over one arm and nodded his head in concession. His heavy hiking boots scuffed over the floor as he turned and moved out the door ahead of Julia.

She cast one apprehensive glance at Craig, who had already begun to feverishly dial phone numbers, then pulled her office door shut with a resounding clunk.

Cameron had taken a few steps away from her and as she turned to face him, she couldn't help noticing the width of his shoulders, the long line of his back and legs.

"This way, please, I prefer to start my tour with the back side." Her face flushed hot as a flame when she realized how he might take that. "I mean, the back side of the building, of course."

"Of course." He twisted his head to look at her from the corner of his eye, keeping his back to her. "What else could you mean, lass?"

She opened her mouth to further explain, then decided not to make an issue out of a simple poor choice of words. "This way."

She pushed ahead, trying to ignore the sheer physical power she felt as she brushed by him in the hallway. Next to him, Julia felt diminutive but not overwhelmed. Not many men she met in her everyday work towered over her tall frame.

Proportion. That's what she felt, as if she and this Cameron were a meant-to-be matched set—but a set of what? Peas in a pod? Love birds? She thought of his allusions that suggested he knew about the gold. Her breath seemed to ball in her lungs and force its way upward as she exhaled. Maybe cat and mouse was a better description.

She hurried down the narrow stairway and hit the swinging gymnasium doors with the full force of her fear. The loud thump echoed in the huge, empty room as the doors whooshed open.

"Years ago, this building housed a prestigious parochial high school." She walked at a brisk pace up the aisle created by rows of metal bunkbeds. "When they consolidated with another school and moved to a new facility, this building was left standing empty. After a time, several local churches bought the place, converting the upstairs classrooms into offices. The downstairs with its gym, cafeteria, and lockers was set up as the shelter."

She drew in the musty odor of the linens, the faint scents of the occupants who had been here only a few hours ago. Her soft-soled shoes slapped against the hard floor as she rushed across the room to push open another swinging door. "Through here, we have the lockers and showers."

"I'm sure those are appreciated." He peered in for an instant just as she released the heavy door and it fell shut.

"We rent the lockers for a nominal fee to the working homeless. It gives us a little bit of revenue and them a place to store their things while they're on the job."

"Working homeless? Can there be such a thing?"

Julia smiled at the rhetorical question that Cameron murmured under his breath.

She led on, steering him back out into the main hallway with a determined stride. "That's the cafeteria. I'll show it to you on the way back."

As if determined to slow her breakneck progress, Cameron stopped to peek through the small rectangular window in one of the doors she had just given a dismissive wave. "'Tis empty."

"Trust me, it doesn't stay empty." She moved on, unwilling to let him drag the tour on a moment longer than necessary. "Hot meals are a big part of our service."

He nodded.

"Still, I have wondered if we'd do better to cut those out in order to utilize that space as a full-time shelter for women with children."

At the end of the hall, she worked the wobbling knob of a heavy, steel door, opening it to reveal a dirty little courtyard and loading dock. "This door is locked at all times except two hours in the morning for deliveries."

She let the door fall shut, pivoted on her heel and headed back toward Cameron. Her pulse drummed like the William Tell Overture in her ears as she raced on to wind up the tour and see him on his way. She slipped past Cameron, her mind on getting through this, then on to her real problems.

Something warm and quite insistent met her arm.

Cameron's hand, curved over the crook in her elbow, stopped her just as she moved to pass him.

Was it the sudden halt of her bum's rush or the nearness of the green-eyed Irish man that made Julia feel as though she'd just stepped off a Tilt-a-Whirl? She angled her chin upward, meeting his gaze with what she hoped could pass for curiosity, not cowardice.

"Excuse me, lass, but did you say children?"

"What?" She felt her brow wrinkle.

"If I heard you right, you said you thought you should use the cafeteria for homeless women with children." He emphasized the last two words with hushed disbelief.

"Yes, I'm afraid that's true. I wish it weren't." She slipped her arm from his distracting grasp.

"Families, without homes? Right here in America?" He shook his head and a lock of golden hair fell against his forehead. "I thought things had gotten so much better. You hardly hear about homelessness on the news anymore."

"And since it's not in the news, it's not on people's minds or in their hearts as much, and so the funding starts to fade and—" She sighed. "At this rate, I don't see how we can keep the existing shelter open, much less add new services."

He scowled, his handsome face cast downward.

Julia seized the opportunity to edge by him, eager to get on with the tour.

"The kitchen is through here." She flattened her palm on the still-warm door of the perpetually hot room. She turned when she sensed he had not followed her.

Seeing him standing a few steps away, just where she had left him, tugged at her heart. "Cameron? Are you all right?"

"I just hadn't expected…" He placed one large hand over his folded parka. "This job is turning out to have facets I hadn't counted on."

She nodded. "You aren't the first volunteer to feel a bit overwhelmed by it all."

And you haven't even gotten into the real nitty gritty of it, she thought. Still, his reaction made her wonder—could it be he was just a good man with the best of intentions? Perhaps she had let her own fear and confusion distort his perfectly innocent comments into innuendoes and threats.

"After a while," she said, mindful that she may have misjudged the man, "you realize you can't solve it all, and you accept that and adapt."

"How can you accept the idea of children saying their bedtime prayers in a converted cafeteria?"

The quiet power of his question spoke straight to her being.

"You can accept something without liking it, with still wanting to change it, Mr. O'Dea." She moved to bridge the few feet between them, her hand reaching out to touch his forearm. "There have always been the poor. I suppose, despite the effort of good people, there always will be."

"Even the Lord Jesus said as much," he murmured, not looking directly at her. "'You will always have the poor among you, but you will not always have me.'"

"As long as the doors to *this* shelter stay open, even the poor will always have him," she whispered, her throat tight with emotion over the idea that the man she had feared might well share her faith. "Or as much of him as this watered-down reflection can offer."

She watched for his reaction. A laugh, a sneer, any scoffing gesture would tell her so much. But she saw none of those in his clear green eyes.

"You're a good woman, Julia Reed. I've heard it said that we are the only gospel some people will ever hear. If that is so, you and your work here make me feel as if my own testimony is nothing more than a faint whisper."

"If that were true, you wouldn't volunteer your time here."

"I wish I could say I'd come out of a calling in my heart or even a sense of Christian duty, but, lass, it simply isn't so."

"I'm not sure I want to hear this." She stepped back. The heel of her shoe banged against the worn brass kickplate of the kitchen door. Her fingertips brushed the old ridges in the wood as she pressed her spine to the sturdy support. She imagined someone pounding on the closed door couldn't make any more noise than the hammering beat of her pulse.

"You see, Miss Reed—" Cameron's feet moved forward on the scarred tile.

"You know, don't you?" She swallowed, and it felt as though she'd forced a walnut-sized lump of foreboding down her throat to plummet hard into the pit of her stomach.

"I know a great deal." Evasiveness to the rescue again. Cameron smoothed his hand over the waterproof fabric of his parka.

He felt bad for not confiding in her, but he couldn't, not yet. First he had to discern just how deep Miss Julia Reed had buried herself in this mess. From what he knew of her on paper and now in person, he suspected she was involved right up to her hairline. Still, he had to have that suspicion confirmed before he divulged anything of his mission.

He cocked his head and notched up the old Irish charm, focusing a wee bit of a smile on the lass as he murmured in a lilting baritone. "What interests me, Julia Reed, woman with a heart after saving the world, is what *you* know."

Fear flickered in the depths of her dilated pupils. Her pale hand went to the neck of her T-shirt, fingers winding in her sweater as she pulled it closed tightly over her throat. She shut her eyes. Her lips moved, not to speak to him, but as if to form words perceptible only between herself and the Lord.

Her hasty prayer, it seemed, gave her strength. When her eyes opened again, she straightened her shoulders. She tipped her face up, her thick hair tumbling back from her face, giving her a regal look.

No, regal wasn't quite it, Cameron decided. She appeared more like a lioness defending her cub when she planted her hands on her hips and spoke with unquestionable authority.

"What I know, Mr. O'Dea, is that if you or your phony-baloney Officer Shaughnessy—"

"Shaughnessy? Michael Shaughnessy?" The name made Cameron's blood run cold. "I wondered if you'd crossed his path. Tell me, how much do you know about him?"

"Only that he isn't a real police officer and that he's the one who took the boy."

"The boy," he echoed. *The boy* was his nephew, Devin, who was now being used as bait.

When Cameron had returned to the billboard, Devin had vanished. Cameron had only been gone twenty minutes or so, just long enough to walk to the nearest pay phone. He'd called for police help in retrieving the gold, then picked up something for the boy to eat—they'd been out all day and the child had been famished.

A late night phone call had informed him that Michael Shaughnessy, a man Cameron had once considered like a brother, had taken Devin hostage. The kidnapper intended to hold the boy until Cameron turned over the gold. Michael hadn't known how close he'd been to nabbing the treasure himself, nor had he mentioned any run-ins with Julia or any other person for that matter.

Greed, it seemed, had made his old friend, and current nemesis, sloppy. That was good news for Cameron and his quest. But Michael's blinding lust for the gold could certainly prove a very dangerous thing for the woman who knew that he had the boy—especially since she had the gold. If she did have the gold.

He narrowed his eyes at her. "So you saw Shaughnessy take the boy?"

"Saw him?" She snuffed out a quick sound of self-disgust. "Mister, I handed the poor child right over to that imposter, and I could just kick myself for doing it, too."

She shifted her gaze, then her demeanor changed. She fixed him with a daggered glare. "But that's nothing compared to what will happen to you and your partner if you harm one red hair on that precocious leprechaun's head."

"Leprechaun?" His voice squeaked on the word so peculiarly thrust into the weighty discussion.

"That was the kid's story, not mine," she hurried to explain.

"He actually told you he was a leprechaun?" Cameron laughed.

"With an accent thick as peat moss and a tale as intricate as Irish lace," she said, her body relaxing just an inch. "He even went so far as to grant me his buried—"

She jerked as if pricked by a pin. She gasped and her fingers went to her lips as if to seal the rest of the sentence in.

Cameron's head snapped up. He pushed forward a step, standing so close that he felt her shallow breathing against the parka wadded between them. "He granted you his buried what? Tell me."

She jerked her head to one side. "The tour is over now, Mr. O'Dea. I'll thank you to be on your way."

"I'm not going anywhere until you tell me." He would not release her from his heated gaze.

"I'm warning you, Mr. O'Dea. If you don't leave this very minute, I'll—"

"What?" He leaned in. Menacing, he supposed, but with a purpose. Still, when he saw the glimmer of distress in those lovely eyes and knew he had been the cause of it, Cameron winced.

"I mean it," she said again with growing fervor. "Leave at once or I'll—I'll scream. One scream from me would draw every person in this building. They'd be on you like that." She snapped her fingers. "And it wouldn't take long then for the police to show up."

"No, Miss Reed, I dare say it wouldn't take long at all." He reached into his back pocket and eased out his billfold. Like all the detectives on all the old TV shows he'd ever seen, he used a sharp flip of his wrist to pop open the leather wallet and flash his shiny gold badge.

Her lips fell open. Her gaze darted from the badge and ID to his face, then back to the ID again.

53

"As you can see, the police are already here," he said, no longer able to try to jiggle the information gently out of a seemingly innocent conversation with her. "Now, why don't you tell nice Special Agent O'Dea what you've done with your pot of leprechaun's gold?"

J ulia, this could only happen to you."

Her shoulders tightened in defense at Craig's gentle ribbing. "What?"

"Only you could go along innocently pursuing your one meager ambition, a simple quest to rescue each and every single lost soul you ever happen to come across—" he wrinkled his nose and lowered his voice, "—and end up with the *Man from U.N.C.L.E.* rifling through your office safe."

"Interpol," came the deep, Irish-accented voice from inside the half-open closet.

"Interpol." Julia echoed Cameron's correction. Her swivel chair groaned as she leaned away from her desk, trying to see how far Cameron had gotten in accounting for all the gold coins.

"Interpol, U.N.C.L.E., po-tay-to, po-tah-to. What's the difference?"

Cameron stood and turned. He braced his forearm against the open closet door and fixed a hard gaze on Craig. "One is a multinational cooperative of police agencies targeting international criminal activity, the other is a work of fiction."

"Which is which?" Craig deadpanned.

"Craig!" They were in enough trouble without her assistant antagonizing the man sent to deal with them.

She bit her lip and glanced at Cameron, forcing a humorless chuckle up from her clenched chest. She'd thought him a powerful man the first moment she'd laid eyes on him. Open and approachable, but capable of taking care of himself, his business, and anyone else who needed it. Now that she knew more about him, her estimation had grown.

She raised her eyes to the imposing figure standing framed in the doorway. "I'm sorry, he didn't mean—"

"That's all right." Cameron held up one hand to cut her apology short. "I understand his protectiveness."

"You do?" Julia tilted her head questioningly.

Cameron's features softened. His deep voice came low and intimate, as if sharing a secret with an old friend. "Yes, pretty Miss Reed, I do. You see, while you're about your Father's business trying to do the work of a hundred angels, your assistant is trying to do the work of only one."

"One?"

"Yours." He nodded solemnly. His gaze flicked toward Craig, then back to Julia. "Your guardian angel, I suspect."

"Look, Blarney Bill, don't start any rumors going around about Julia and me." Craig bristled, his bony shoulders taut. He dragged his fingers back through his hair. "I have a girlfriend, thank you very much. I'm just looking out for Julia."

The dazzling green eyes shifted to meet the narrowed gaze of her assistant. Cameron tipped his head, acknowledging Craig's behavior, perhaps even admiring it. "As well you should. You've already had one mishap with a counterfeit police officer. Fool me once, shame on you. Fool me twice—"

"And bang, you're dead." Craig wound his arms over his chest. "That's how serious this is, isn't it, O'Dea?"

Julia stiffened. Cameron soothed her jangled nerves with a single, focused glance. "You're safe, Miss Reed. Let me assure you of that."

"But for how long?" Craig stubbed the toe of his shoe against the desk leg. "People have done some pretty awful things for a lot less than what's in that safe. When this Shaughnessy comes looking for Julia, it won't be to dance a little jig."

"He's already taken your nephew." Emotion made Julia's usually strong voice fade to a faraway whisper. Cameron had told her the quick story of how he had taken a leave of absence from his work to try to find the gold once and for all. When he and his twelve-year-old nephew had followed a very improbable clue, they stumbled onto the gold. After reburying the coins, Cameron went to call for police backup. Shaughnessy had been posing as a police officer all over the city to keep tabs on O'Dea and had apparently intercepted the dispatch request on a police scanner.

Julia cleared her throat and managed to speak a little louder. "He knows I'm a witness to kidnapping, even if he doesn't realize I found the gold."

"As I explained, Shaughnessy didn't know we'd actually found the gold. I just asked for assistance of the police. I intended to get my nephew out of there, then post a guard as I dug the gold up again."

"But—" Julia scraped her teeth over her bottom lip. "What if Shaughnessy makes your nephew tell him?"

Pain and guilt flashed in Cameron's green eyes at that suggestion. "He wouldn't dare harm the boy."

"But he might dare harm Julia," Craig argued like a dog with a bone.

"Especially if he puts two and two together and concludes that I unearthed the coins." She was thinking aloud more than giving voice to any fears. "It wouldn't take a genius to figure that out."

"Yeah. You did," Craig muttered to the tall man dominating the room.

"Shaughnessy won't get to Miss Reed." Cameron's voice rose with authority.

"How can you be so sure?" Craig raised an eyebrow.

"Because I won't let him."

The hard, no-nonsense phrase hung in the air like a noxious vapor.

The three waited, each eyeing the other. No one wanted to break the brittle silence. The tension around them charged the dry air so that it felt as if one sound might set off a spark that could ignite an explosion of emotion.

Julia's heartbeat throbbed in her temples and thudded in her ears. Her hands tangled in her lap, winding tighter and tighter together until her skin burned and her knuckles ached.

Cameron's gaze held steady, unyielding.

Finally, she had to say something. "I put my faith in the Lord, Mr. O'Dea, not in any one man."

"You're a wise woman," he said, a hint of a smile at the corner of his lips.

"But I have learned that there comes a time when I must place my trust in someone." She stood and faced him, her arms folding over her chest as if that could still her pounding heart. "You're that someone, Mr. O'Dea. Tell me what we have to do to get your nephew back safely."

Shortly before noon, Cameron pulled his car up to the shelter again. Once he had obtained Julia's cooperation in this adventure gone awry, he'd had to act fast. First he'd had to spirit away the gold and place it in a place both secret and secure. Only he and his direct supervisor knew the hideaway. That made Julia useless to Michael as a guide to the treasure. Nothing he had learned about or sensed from Julia made him think she would reveal anything. But he also could not take the chance that she might give the location away by accident or out of some misplaced idea that her involvement could turn the tables for Devin.

Then, he'd had to gather all the information and equipment he would need for the mission. He'd already made one slip up going in unprepared. He would not be so careless again.

He rubbed his tired eyes with his thumb and forefinger. Sleep had evaded him last night. But then, he doubted he would rest much at all until Devin and that gold were safely where they belonged.

The car door let out a long metallic creak as he nudged it open with his shoulder. He'd hoped Julia would be waiting for him on the sidewalk outside St. Patrick's. She'd promised to give him a full hour of her precious time to go over things with him in her office, with Craig Davis lurking about, no doubt.

Cameron had insisted they meet outside the shelter over lunch—an invitation he did not extend to her assistant.

Julia's reticence to spend time alone with him had prompted him to include Devin's mother in the meeting. It was good for Fiona to get out instead of waiting and worrying by the phone. It also saved him the trouble of repeating his plan separately to both women. Besides, the last thing he wanted today was to spend his meal with Craig's beady-eyed gaze boring holes into his head.

Cameron checked his watch. If Julia didn't show up in a couple of minutes, he'd have to go in and drag her away from the latest emergency good deed that she thought only she could attend to. He had to smile at her tenacity and go-get-'em attitude, but he wondered if she didn't get weary trying to take on so much. And now he and his little family scandal had added to her workload.

He drummed his fingers on the roof of his sedan, tempted to march inside and tell Julia he didn't need her help after all. The nerve-jangling trill of his brand new cellular phone kept him from doing it. He'd hated to succumb to the tyranny of always carrying a phone with him, but he couldn't help thinking if he'd had one yesterday when he and Devin had gone off adventuring, all would be well right now. He slid back behind the wheel and flipped open the phone.

"O'Dea here," he answered.

"Uncle Cam?"

"Devin!" He gripped the phone receiver so hard the plastic cut into his palm. "Devin, lad, where are you?"

"Now, you know I can't be lettin' him tell you that, Cam, old man."

Michael Shaughnessy's voice dripped sarcasm and contempt through the phone line.

The sound brought a weighty chill to the pit of Cameron's stomach. "How did you get this number, Michael?"

"We called Mom first, Uncle Cam. She gave it to us. I hope it's okay."

"Of course it's okay," Shaughnessy chimed in. "Your Uncle Cam just loves hearing from you, son—just as I'd love to hear from him. Especially if he has gold news—I mean *good* news for me."

"I'm telling you, Michael, if you lay one hand on that boy—"

"I'm okay, Uncle Cam. Uncle Mike understands that I don't know where the gold is and he isn't pushing me to tell him anything."

"I see." The knot in his stomach eased a bit.

"It's just like being on one of those fishing trips he used to take me on," Devin chattered, oddly chipper. "Except no fish."

"No fish?" Though his heart wasn't in it, Cameron needed to find a way to comfort the boy, to make things seem under control. "That's not so different from your usual fishing trips."

Fishing trips. Cameron's mind raced as the boy laughed at his lame joke. Was Devin giving him a hint as to their whereabouts? He made a mental note to have every nearby pond and camping area checked. Michael would not get too far from the gold at this stage, Cameron was sure.

"I just don't want you to worry about me, Uncle Cam. Uncle Mike let me talk to Mom a long time and she knows I'm okay," Devin went on.

Another mental note. *Quiz Fiona on her conversation with Devin and get a tape recorder and a tracing device on her phone ASAP.*

"Devin, I want you to know, I will do everything I can to get you home to your Mom as soon as possible."

"Everything?" A slippery quality permeated Michael's tone. "Does that include handing over you-know-what?"

Cameron clamped his jaw down so tight he could hear his back teeth grind together.

"Well, Cam?" Michael pushed.

"You know I don't have the gold, Michael." Not on him, at least.

"But when you get it—and that will be soon, I suspect—I wonder if you'd be willing to part with it in exchange for Devin's safe return?"

Devin's safe return. The evil implications pricked at Cameron's imagination. "So that's it, then. You've officially reduced yourself to threatening your own godson—the child you swore you would love and protect as your own flesh and blood. And for what, Michael? Money? Fulfillment of some legend based on a kind of twisted logic?"

"I would never hurt Devin. Never."

Deep in his heart, Cameron trusted the vehemence of that claim. He had to cling to the hope that the Michael he had once known and loved like his own brother would keep that promise. He had to try to reach that man. "Then let Devin go, Michael. Keep this between you and me."

"It can never just be between the two of us, Cam, and you know it. It's for Devin I'm doing this, for his future."

"Devin's future does not lie in that gold."

"I think otherwise, and when you find it—"

"*If* I find it," Cameron corrected.

"*When* you find it. You will find it. I know you're close now. That's why, when I saw my opportunity to take Devin, I didn't hesitate. I knew you were closing in on the treasure and I needed an edge. I didn't do it to hurt the boy."

"It hurts him to be away from his mother."

"Then find the gold so he can go home to her." A detached frostiness tinged Michael's words.

Cameron shuddered to realize that the corruption of his old friend had run so deep. "What are you going to do in the meantime?"

Michael laughed. "Just keep enjoying my little *fishing* expedition, I suppose."

"Let Devin go," he urged again, praying his appeal would not go unheeded.

"Find the gold."

Cameron closed his eyes against the searing pain of his failure to touch the soul of his former friend.

"Oh, and Cam," Michael added, his voice lowering, "I've been one step behind for a long time, old man. So don't be too surprised if, just as you reach down to snatch up one of those beautiful golden coins, 'tis my shadow that falls across your back."

The loud click stung Cameron's ear.

'Tis my shadow that falls across your back. It sounded like a threat. Michael was threatening him. Devin might be safe with the man, but was anyone else? Could Michael have sunk so low he would harm Cameron? And what danger was Julia in now?

"Now I know how a worm feels when it's dangling from a fish-hook."

"Quit squirming, lass, or you'll know how a worm feels when it gets stuck on a fishhook." Cameron closed the sharp pin into the latch, then leaned back in the driver's seat of his car to admire the small golden pin he'd placed on her sweater. "Besides, you're not the bait in this little plan of mine, I am."

"If I'm not the bait, then why are you tagging me like some animal about to be released into the wild?" She pressed her chin to her chest to get a glimpse of the pin.

"It's just a tiny tracking device." Cameron held the tracking receiver in the palm of his hand. A whisk and several muted clicks filled the air as he whipped up the high tech gizmo's antenna. He pointed it toward the pin and a green light went berserk with blinking. He turned the wiggling sensor away from the pin and on came a steady red light. "Everything seems to be in order. Don't worry."

"An agent of Interpol is about to monitor my every move-ment just in case I fall into the clutches of some loony with lep-rechaun gold fever and you say don't worry." She batted her eyes at him. "Any other advice?"

The wind teased her long curls through the barely open car window. The brisk late-winter breeze brought a glow to her cheeks and a sparkle to her eyes. Behind her, along the busy street outside his favorite Cincinnati restaurant, the noon lunch crowd shuffled and scurried in the bright sunlight, oblivious to the secret goings-on in the nondescript brown sedan.

Cameron did not feel such detachment. Already in his quest to clear his family name, he had placed an innocent loved one at risk—and that person had gotten snared in the process. He would not let Julia fall victim to his carelessness as Devin had.

An icy cold filled the bottom of his stomach, a gloomy fog shrouded his thoughts. Why hadn't he sent Devin home first, then returned to see if they'd actually found the hiding spot of the gold? He told himself he hadn't really believed the gold could lie in such an obvious place, but his heart knew—and God knew as well—that impatience had won out. Pride had won out. Even greed, not to possess the money, but to seize his goal at long last, had won out.

Even though he knew that Michael Shaughnessy would never hurt Devin, for he loved the boy like a son and was, in fact, the boy's godfather, Cameron's remorse over his actions ate away at him.

Julia scowled at the tracking device, her full lips pursed in a pout.

Cameron had to laugh. "Don't be such a skeptic. It will work."

"That's what I'm afraid of, that you'll have cause to use it."

"It's a precaution."

"So are locks and bolts and all manner of self-defense devices. That doesn't mean I have to be happy I live in a place where they're necessary." She crossed her arms.

"Well, if you can't be happy, could you at least be hungry? Because I'm ready for lunch." He jerked his thumb toward the double doors of the restaurant.

Julia ducked her head to check out the place, moving her folded arms lower to cover her flat stomach. "I think I'll just sit and drink a glass of water while you eat."

"Oh, but you have to try the food here. It's excellent."

"No, really. All the excitement today and waiting to hear the rest of your plan about how to catch Shaughnessy, it's kind of squashed my appetite. I couldn't eat a bite."

A low, growling complaint from the depths of her belly contradicted her claim.

"Oh, you couldn't?" he asked, pretending not to hear the grumblings. "You're sure, not even a bite? Perhaps something light?"

She shook her head. "I can't."

"They make a Caesar salad here with grilled chicken—or you can have it with plump, juicy shrimp instead. And the fresh bread, piping hot, dripping with sweet butter—"

"I said I couldn't eat a thing."

Her eyes, the flare of her nostrils, the delicate way her tongue danced over the part in her lips—as though she could taste the delicious fare already—said otherwise. And if that weren't enough, her stomach chimed in again.

"You can't eat or you won't? You're not on some crazy diet, are you?"

"No!" Her shoulders pulled up like a defensive cat's. "Though I could certainly stand to lose a few—"

"Don't you dare." He made a show of sweeping his gaze over her without appearing lascivious. "You're a fine, healthy girl. You look perfect just as you are. And I won't be sitting at a table with you, me enjoying a hearty lunch and you sippin' on water."

"Then perhaps we should move this little executive planning meeting of yours elsewhere because I'm not ordering one bite of food." She huffed and turned her profile to him.

"We can't go somewhere else. I've already arranged for Devin's mother to meet us here." He tucked the tracking receiver into the inner pocket of his parka and raked his fingers back through the springy hair along his temple. "You're eating and I'll say no more of it."

"I am not and I'll listen to no more of it." Her long legs angled in his direction. She wriggled in her seat, her breathing controlled but hard as she spoke through her clenched teeth. "I agreed to work with you, Mr. O'Dea, not to take orders from you without question."

He lowered his voice to a dangerous whisper. "There'll be times, lass, when you'll for sure take an order from me without question. The success of this mission may well depend on it."

"I understand that, but I also understand this is not one of those times." She poked one finger into her cupped palm. "The success of your precious mission, my friend, hardly rests on my scarfing down a chicken Caesar salad here when I have a perfectly good peanut butter sandwich back at the shelter."

He rolled his eyes. He admired frugality as much as the next good steward, but she took it a bit too far. "Pity you didn't bring your little lunch pail with you then, lass."

"Well, I would have if I had known you planned a meeting in a restaurant where I can't even afford an appetizer."

Boom. The revelation dropped like a frozen hailstone in the heated discussion.

"Oh." He nodded. "So that's how it is, is it?"

A blush blossomed on her cheeks as she bit her lip.

"Well, don't you be worrying about that, lass. I can well afford—"

"No." She held her hand up. "I can't let you pay for my lunch."

"And why not?"

"Because you're a man and I'm a woman and it might look like a date or something."

He shifted in his seat, laying one forearm over the steering wheel. He studied her intently. "And that would be the worst horror in the world, for you and I to go on a date?"

"We have a working relationship, Mr. O'Dea."

"Cameron."

"Mr. O'Dea."

Her gaze locked to his like iron to a magnet. Their wills were more like iron to iron. He smiled as he recalled the verse in Proverbs: "iron sharpens iron."

He had a feeling that once his time with Julia Reed had ended, they'd both be as keen-edged as any saber.

ᴥ 5 ᴧ

ameron Brennan William O'Dea! How can you, in good
conscience, sit at this table, two meals before you and Miss
Reed with only a wee bit o' water to stave her hunger off?"
Fiona O'Dea picked up her fork and pretended to jab at the
brother of her late husband.

"What can I say, Fiona, my darling?" Cameron spread his
arms as wide as the curved booth would allow. "I'm a glutton."

"A glutton for punishment, you are, for carrying on so in
front of me." She shook her pixie-short red hair back from her
freckled face. "If I were you, Miss Reed, that man'd be wearing
that second grilled chicken Caesar salad as a hat, he would."

"I'm telling you, Fiona, when I ordered, I didn't realize the
salads would be so—" He waved his hand back and forth over
the dishes.

The smell of the rich dressing and the marinated and grilled
bits of white chicken wafted over Julia. The gnawing ache in
her belly deepened.

"Bountiful," Cameron concluded. "I suppose I just got carried away."

"And you'll be carrying away one of those salads, I'm sup-posin', as well, since you certainly can't eat them both now."

He shook his head and clicked his tongue in dismay over the mouthwatering food. "Unfortunately, Caesar salad with the dressing already on it doesn't keep well. Does not keep well at all." He plunged his fork into the crisp bed of dark, leafy spinach. "If only there were a way to keep it from going to waste."

He used his fork to gesture as he went on, pushing a bite of smoke-scented chicken and hearty greens, shimmering with dressing and sprinkled with pungent parmesan cheese, practically under Julia's nose. "Can you think of a way to keep this delicious food from going to waste, Miss Reed?"

Her eyes followed the swaying path of the fork. She sighed.

"You can eat it, Miss Reed," Fiona suggested, pushing the bowl toward Julia.

"Now, why didn't I think of that?" Cameron slapped the heel of his hand against his forehead.

Julia rolled her eyes and shook her head, directing her gaze heavenward. "How on earth does a man who is such a lousy actor make a living as a secret agent?"

"I'm not a secret agent."

Her lips twitched, fighting against the urge to break into a grin. "But you are a lousy actor."

"Does that mean you'll indulge my little pretense here and eat the salad, lass?" He picked up the fork beside her and offered it.

She considered the gleaming silver utensil and the gesture. "Well—okay."

"Good." Cameron pushed the second bowl of salad fully in front of her.

She placed her hand on his wrist. "But I want to make it crystal clear that I'm only accepting this meal because you've already paid for it."

"I understand," he murmured.

"And it would be wrong to let it go to waste out of a sense of foolish pride," she said firmly.

"I understand," he repeated.

"And because, Mr. Cameron Brennan William O'Dea—" She moved in closer, so close she could see the golden-tipped fringe of his lashes around his emerald eyes. "In regard to your comment earlier today, I do always tell the truth."

He blinked. "I don't understand."

She lifted her hand from his. Giving a quick salute with the shiny fork, she cocked her head and answered, "I have to admit it, I'm hungry. And that's the truth."

The conversation veered from one topic to another as they ate. Fiona kept chatting with a lively pace that surprised Julia. She supposed it was what was commonly referred to as a good front. Only the tension around the woman's sometimes wincing smile gave evidence of the fear and pain beneath the calm exterior.

"I guess we can't put it off any longer, Fiona," Cameron finally said. "We need to talk about Michael—and Devin—and what we need to do next."

"Whatever it is, Cam, tell me it will bring Devin home safely—and soon." She drummed her short nails on the tablecloth. "I promised him he wouldn't be gone long when we spoke today."

"I need to ask you about that," he said, taking her hand in his. "I need to know everything that was said. Did Devin give any indication where he might be?"

"None." She lowered her gaze.

"What about the rest of the conversation?" He prodded gently, aware of her fragile state, but not wanting to miss anything that might aid his search for the boy.

"There isn't much to tell." She raised her shoulders, then let them fall in heavy resignation. "We spoke a moment about missin' one another and about how soon we'd be together. He told me his Uncle Mike was looking fine well after him."

"And fishing?" Cameron wet his lips and narrowed one eye at her. "Did he mention anything about fishing?"

Her red-brown eyebrows angled downward over her perplexed gaze. "Fishing?"

"You don't think Shaughnessy has taken your nephew fishing, do you?" Julia asked.

Cameron lifted his shoulders, feeling the tenseness in his muscles beneath the coarse wool of his sweater. "It's just something Devin said to me, that it was like going on a fishing trip with his Uncle Mike."

"True enough," Fiona added as she squinted thoughtfully toward the restaurant door. "They did go off fishing plenty o' times. Sometimes in the summer for a week or more."

Her gaze moved to Cameron's face. "Now that you mention it, Devin told me, 'Just pretend, Mom, that I'm off early on spring break with Uncle Mike, just like we planned.'"

"He had a trip planned with Michael for spring break?" Cameron asked.

Fiona nodded. "He talked about it almost to the point of obsession. 'Twas the only thing I've seen Michael excited about except that blasted treasure in a long time. If I hadn't known better, I'd have thought there was some connection."

"Do you think there was?" Cameron pulled a small notebook from the parka slung over the back of the booth. He flipped open the pad and began making notations, starting with the word *gold*, double underlined and in capital letters.

"Michael never let on that there was. He did say that if he didn't have the gold by then he was going on this trip."

"Did he say anything else? Think carefully, Fiona."

She narrowed one eye. "Michael said he needed to go there—to see for himself. Oh, and here's a direct quote: he said he'd grown tired of trying to 'wait him out'—him being you, of course."

Cameron's pen made a deep indention as he wrote "wait him out."

"I assumed he meant this was a much-needed vacation. Still, when he talked of it his eyes got all wild. That's why I didn't want Devin to go."

"Where?"

Fiona shut her eyes and gave out a weary sigh. "Not far. A place Michael said he had to go, to see it for himself. Cumberland Falls, Kentucky."

"Cumberland Falls? Isn't that the place Da was wanting us all to visit before the accident?" He made note of the name.

"Yes, your father did speak of it often. He said sometime when you were in the area for a visit, we'd all of us go."

Thoughts of his late father, and with him his only brother, weighed heavy on Cameron. But that only reinforced his need to get Devin home soon. He pressed on with his questions. "You said earlier that Michael said he needed to see for himself—see what for himself?"

"The moonbow."

"The moonbow?" He scribbled down the strange word.

She folded her hands on the table. "'Tis a natural phenomenon that appears over the waterfall come the full moon."

"Full moon," he muttered as he copied it down.

"It just so happened that Devin's spring break coincided with the very next occurrence of the moonbow." She smiled. "There was a part of me that found the very idea of that almost too charming to resist myself."

"But you hadn't agreed that Michael could take Devin?" Julia asked insistently.

Cameron scowled at her to imply she had begun to tread on family business.

73

"Excuse me for butting in," she said. "But my experience in social service makes me ask. Do you realize that the kidnapping charge might be nullified if Fiona gave Michael permission for a trip?"

"Of course I didn't give Michael permission to snatch my child, or to take him anywhere." Fire flashed in Fiona's eyes. "These last few weeks I haven't allowed Devin to go off at all with Michael. With all this gold nonsense building up so, I didn't feel right about it."

"So, you'd say the gold adds an element of danger to the situation?" Julia acknowledged Cameron's none too subtle throat-clearing with a glance. "I wouldn't ask, but I do know how best to proceed in cases of child welfare and having all the facts could make a critical difference."

"'Tis a curse on this family, that gold is." Fiona hissed the last words, spilling out her anger against the source of her trouble.

"It and all the hoopla that surrounded it," Cameron agreed, patting his sister-in-law on the back.

"Hoopla?" Julia raised her brows.

Cameron pressed his back to the seat. The soft cushion sighed with the shift in weight. "Fifty years ago, Michael Shaughnessy's grandfather and my own robbed a private treasure—a chest of antique gold coins, the ill-gotten gain of a very corrupt official."

"For a time they thought they might get away with it, but then the truth began to come to light," Fiona explained.

"My grandfather talked too much, bragged on and on." Cameron tapped his hiking boot against the table leg, wishing he could keep the old anger from swelling within his chest. "Michael's grandfather escaped to America only to be deported for the crime soon after. Both of them died in prison."

"Well, that explains how it got here from Ireland." Julia tilted her head to one side. "But what about the 'hoopla'?"

"Some saw the robbery, not as an act of thievery and avarice, but as a political statement, a means of common man's justice." Cameron rubbed one hand along his cheek. "My grandfather became something of a local legend, his woeful story told in pubs and passed from father to son these past fifty years. Michael, my brother, and I grew up in our small town with that as our legacy."

"Your grandfathers had become folk heroes? Like Robin Hood?" Julia asked.

Cameron barked out a sharp laugh. "Those men were no heroes."

"To your father they were, and to Michael Shaughnessy." Fiona lay both hands on the table. "But I don't want him to become one to Devin."

"How so?" Julia drew a long strand of black hair over her shoulder and leaned forward.

"What with Michael filling my son's mind with wild stories of family glory and rightful ownership of those coins." One of Fiona's hands drew into a weak fist.

"Those tales have turned many a young boy's head," said Cameron. "My own father, in a misplaced sense of loyalty, kept the secret of the gold's whereabouts from everyone until he thought it 'safe' for the family to cash in on the treasure."

"Unfortunately he—and my husband—were killed right here in Cincinnati in a traffic accident last year." Fiona rubbed one fingertip along the brim of her water glass. "My father-in-law had been the one to work out the paperwork to get us here from Ireland two years ago, but we did not know why until later."

"What an amazing story," Julia whispered.

Cameron nodded. "In going through my father's things after his funeral, I discovered several clues. But none as vital as his last words, which haunt me still."

"What were they?" Julia asked in hushed kindness.

Cameron dipped his gaze downward. "I asked straight out where to find the gold and he said, 'Where would you be thinkin' to find a pot o' gold, man?'"

"At the end of a rainbow," Julia murmured.

"Exactly." He sat back, his head high. "I've devoted as much time as my work would allow to tracing the gold in order to return it and release my family from the burden."

He dragged a breath, filled with the swirling aromas of neighboring lunches, into his lungs. "I've followed any clues— many of them red herrings—one by one, always with Michael on my heels, until I reached that billboard last night."

He exhaled, closing his eyes against the wave of obligation he felt for his nephew's plight. His jaw clenched and his lips formed words he hardly realized he spoke aloud. "What was I thinking? It's all my fault. All my fault."

"No, now none of that." Fiona gave his shoulder a shake.

If he hadn't seen her hand on his arm he would not have known it was there. The stabbing pain tore at his heart. He could scarcely swallow.

"You only intended the best, Cameron." Fiona squeezed his arm. "You meant to provide a male role model for Devin—a better alternative to Michael. I don't blame you."

"I never should have—"

"That doesn't change things, Cameron." Fiona's voice grew raspy with emotion. "Let's just focus on what can be done to bring Devin back to me, where he belongs."

He nodded.

"This gold has taken too heavy a toll on the O'Dea family." Fiona tossed her napkin onto the table like a warrior throwing down a gauntlet. "You've paid too dear a price already, Cameron. I won't see your sorrow added to by letting you heap pointless guilt on yourself."

Julia gave him a veiled glance, a curious look in her eyes. But he couldn't explain to her, not yet.

Cameron waved his hand in the air, as if to physically wipe away the conversation. "It will all be done soon enough, with Miss Reed's cooperation."

"I'll help any way I can," Julia said. "But first, you have to tell me what to do."

"Nothing."

"Nothing?" She blinked at him in disbelief.

"Nothing yet. You see, Devin hasn't let on that I have the gold. Michael thinks we're still searching. We need a way to lure him out alone so I can nab him."

"Why not just tell him you know where the gold is, and when he comes to that place, just grab him?" Julia made it sound so simple.

"Because he's too smart and too suspicious to fall for that." Cameron swept his hand back over his hair, the resilient curls springing against his palm. "Michael would never believe I would just let him have the gold. And if he did show up, that's when we would find ourselves in the most danger."

Both women watched him, their eyes large with anxious anticipation.

"We have to let Michael think that he is still tailing me, that through me he still has a chance of swooping down and taking the gold right out from under my nose."

"And how will you do that?" Julia asked.

"We whet his greed," Cameron replied quietly.

"How?" Fiona wrung her small pale hands.

"I'll have to use the shelter as a cover. I wish there were another way." He underscored his apologetic tone by laying his hand on Julia's arm. "I don't know how else to flush Michael out and keep an eye on you."

Julia brushed her fingertips over the gold pin he'd fastened to her sweater. "But what will you do at the shelter? I'm too busy to have you underfoot."

"Well, when I'm not busy protecting your pretty neck, I think I'd make an excellent volunteer supervisor, strictly on a volunteer basis, of course."

Her eyes grew wide at the suggestion. "I supervise the volunteers."

"And I wouldn't mind seeing what I can do to increase donations and contributions as well," he said, ignoring her response.

"But I oversee that, too." A little-girl-lost quality invaded her soft voice.

"Great, it's settled then." He clapped his hands together.

Julia glowered at him.

He repaid her with a grin.

"At least let me do something to help," Julia insisted. "I have friends in the Kentucky tourism department—we've done some things for the shelter just over the river. I can confirm this whole moonbow story with a phone call and get pamphlets and any information you need sent up."

"Fine. See to it straight away." He tore off the page and handed it to her. He watched as she mocked his authoritarian attitude, mouthing his words back to him, but decided he had that coming and didn't pursue it. Instead, he turned to his sister-in-law.

"Fiona, this may take some time. Several days, maybe more than a week." He cradled Fiona's chin in his cupped palm. "I'm asking you to believe God will watch over Devin, and that he'll help me to do my best to end this for our family once and for all. Can you do that, my dear?"

"I can live on faith for a while, Cameron. But does it make me seem weak to say I'll pray every minute of every day that Michael will come to his senses and let Devin come home to me?"

"It's sometimes when we are our weakest that God does his best work." Cameron tweaked her cheek.

"'I can do all things through Christ the Lord who strengthens me,'" Julia quoted, as she folded Cameron's note.

The petite redhead smiled at both of them. There were tears in her eyes, but she smiled just the same.

Cameron took Julia back to the shelter, then spent the afternoon trying to find where he was most needed in the scheme of things. When it was time for Julia to head home, he suggested he escort her.

She soundly refused his offer.

He followed her home just the same.

"*Now* what do you think you're doing?" Julia slammed her car door and the whole chassis shuddered from the vibrations.

"Can a man help it if he happens to take a drive along the self-same route that a lovely lady motorist is taking?" Cameron leaned his head out the open window of his unremarkable sedan.

"Have you ever noticed, my fine Irish friend—" Julia jabbed the tip of her car key in his direction as she spoke, "—that you answer a lot of questions without ever giving an answer at all?"

"Is that so, lass?" He said it as if the concept had only just struck him. "Well, I'll be."

"I just bet you'll be. I bet you'll be coming up with some fine rare excuse for why it is you'd be wandering down the very lane that winds past me most humble abode." She slipped into the Irish brogue with ease after hearing so much of it recently.

Cameron grinned. "I was sightseeing."

"The sight being the back of my car?"

"Your car, my Miss Reed, is not a sight, it's an eyesore." He popped the door open and began to climb out. "Your home, on the other hand—"

"Is my home." She held up her hand to still any notions he

had of getting any closer to her or her house. "It's where I escape for a while from the stress of my work. And I want it to stay that way—private."

"You're telling me you never invite, say, a friend, over to enjoy your private sanctuary?" He sank back into the driver's seat but did not close the car door.

"Oh, sure, a *friend*." She crossed her arms, hoping that would cement her resolve not to let the man wheedle his way into her home.

She liked Cameron. Liked him more than she had any man in a very long while. But even if she had time for a romantic relationship, he could not be the man for her.

He was an Interpol agent, a traveler, a man essentially without a home of his own. She needed more from a relationship than Cameron could give. And he deserved more than she could offer right now.

"So, you're sayin' we can't be friends?" He cocked his head.

"No." She was saying they could not be more than friends. If she spent too much time with the Irish charmer, she didn't know how to keep that from happening. "I just, well, I just don't want my home invaded."

"Invaded?" He raised an eyebrow.

She lightly touched the pin he'd given her. The cool evening breeze tossed a long coil of hair across the bridge of her nose, and she drew it away as she spoke. "I don't want my privacy invaded."

"I see." He pulled the door quietly shut.

"It's not you. It's me. After working all day at the shelter, I need the solitude of being alone."

"Of course, lass." He gave a gracious bow of his head. "I'll see you in the morning, then."

"Fine." She gave a wave, her wrist rigid and her fingers straight. Suddenly, she felt ridiculously like some royal personage stiffly shooing off a peasant. "In the morning then."

Her afterthought, which she intended to sound cheery, failed miserably and ended up completing the dour dismissal. She felt her cheeks warm at her silly behavior.

Cameron gave a wincing smile.

What was wrong with her? She curled her fingers over the edge of her cardigan. What could it hurt to invite the man in, maybe order a pizza or just sit and talk?

"Until we meet tomorrow," he said, and raised his hand in farewell.

How could she send off such a nice man like this? She wet her lips, ready to renege on her whole stance and ask the man in.

Before she could speak, he raised his wrist to aim one pointed finger at her. "But don't you go thinkin' you can chase me off this easy every time."

"What?" She hadn't seen this shift in attitude coming.

"If I thought 'twas necessary, your foolish stubbornness wouldn't run me off. I'd be over your doorstep, invasion of privacy or no."

Foolish stubbornness? She pulled her shoulders up. "Over my doorstep and then on your way, is what you'd be."

He blinked at her in surprise.

"Pow," she added, stealing from the old Jackie Gleason routine, her loosely knotted fist raised for effect. "Straight to the moon."

He chuckled.

She bit her lip to keep from joining in.

"Thanks for the warning, lass, I'm shakin' in me boots." He let the comfortable lilt saturate his words, then dropped his voice to a serious growl. "In the morning, lass. Bright and early."

Julia watched him drive away, unable to find the breath to voice her anger at his parting command.

∼ 6 ∼

"M y, don't you look chipper this morning?" Julia squinted into the bathroom mirror, then dropped her gaze to the glob of creamy moisturizer in her cupped hand.

The only way that thick pink goo was going to improve the image facing her was if she smeared the stuff directly onto the mirror. Nothing short of blurring the reflection would obscure the evidence of her restless night. This little unplanned treasure escapade would probably age her ten years, she decided.

She rubbed her palms together briskly. The friction warmed the moisturizer and released the delicate scent of vanilla into the air. Julia inhaled deeply, then slathered the cream over her face. Then she grabbed her toothbrush and the tube of toothpaste.

"In the morning, lass. Bright and early." She mimicked Cameron's words as she applied the minty gel to the brush. "What presumption. What arrogance. What—on earth am I doing?"

She glanced down at the huge blue blob quivering on the bristles, then at the tube, which had been crumpled into a ball by her hand. The biting scent of mint stung her nostrils. She sighed, then poked the whole mess into her mouth.

Might as well look as rabid as I feel, she thought in good humor. She attacked the task with enthusiasm until a pale blue froth foamed out over her lips.

She rinsed once and mindlessly started to go at it again, her thoughts focused on Cameron O'Dea and his assumption that she would allow him to run roughshod over her life.

Buzzz-buzzz.

The harsh electric hum of her doorbell startled her back to the moment.

"Well, speak o' the devil," she told her image, pirating Cameron's soft brogue despite the toothbrush stuffed inside her cheek. Her first instinct was to rinse again and tidy her appearance before answering the door.

She resisted it.

Yes, she knew she looked a fright. But that man deserved the fright of his life for showing up on her doorstep so early in the morning.

The doorbell sounded again, and she padded toward the door in her fuzzy slippers. She felt no reservation about appearing in her huge flannel robe belted over a pair of jogging pants and a long T-shirt. Still, she glanced down to make sure all was decent.

Her eyes paused on the pin Cameron had given her with the instruction to wear it at all times. That man, she decided as she jerked her robe over the tracking device, had somehow started to wriggle his way into every aspect of her life. And she didn't like it one bit.

Time to teach that big buttinski a lesson, she thought. An instant before she lunged forward to nab the doorknob, she bent at the waist and shook her head furiously to ensure her hair looked properly wild and woolly.

She chomped down tight on her toothbrush, set her face in

a groggy scowl, then yanked open the front door. "What is it?"

"That's what I'm asking myself." Cameron reached out to push aside the mass of black hair curtaining her face. "What is it?"

She swatted his hand away. "It's someone who has been disturbed far too early in the morning."

"She speaks and the words fall like pearls from her rosy lips." He placed one open hand over his heart.

She rolled her eyes at his attempt to tease her into a better mood.

"You certainly have a glow about you this morning, Miss Reed." He stepped inside the house like an honest-to-goodness invited guest. "I can't quite put my finger on what it is. You're doing your hair differently, aren't you?"

Julia let the front door fall shut with a window-rattling thud. She pulled the toothbrush from her mouth and folded her arms over her chest. "It's a little bit early in the day for me to be apologizing for my looks, friend."

"Oh?" He tipped his head to the right and smiled, revealing just the hint of a dimple. "At what time of day do you usually start apologizing for your looks?"

Apparently he'd missed the hint that she refused to be cajoled out of her sour mood. She eyed him from the top of his tousled hair to his gray wool sweater to the baggy wrinkles around the knees of his jeans. "Very clever remark coming from someone wearing the same outfit he had on yesterday."

"I say if a look works for a fellow, then go with it." He adjusted his thick green parka over one shoulder. "It's a fashion statement."

"And it's screaming 'I sleep in my clothes.'" She shoved the toothbrush back into her mouth and began to scrub with vigor. *Gray sweater? Slept in his clothes? Same outfit?* If her morning became any more cartoonish than it already was, a great big lightbulb would appear over her head.

She pulled the toothbrush out again and used it to point at Cameron in accusation. "You did sleep in your clothes, didn't you? Where were you? Parked in your car outside my house or some such nonsense?"

"Careful with that thing, it's loaded," Cameron said, whisking the back of his hand down his sweater to flick away the spray of tiny white bubbles that had been flung from her toothbrush.

"Give me a straight answer for once, Cameron, or I may just use that fine woolen sweater for a face towel." She swiped the sleeve of her robe along one side of her mouth. "Did you or did you not spend the night on a stakeout outside my house?"

He placed his hands on his hips. "Well, someone has to look out for you."

"I've managed to take care of myself just fine without the intervention of Interpol up till now, thank you." She tucked her toothbrush in her robe pocket and gathered her thick hair back in one hand. "I venture to say I can bumble along a bit longer on my own."

"Bumble being the operative word, I assume."

"If that's supposed to make me laugh—"

"It's supposed to make you *think*."

"Oh, I'm thinking all right. I'm a veritable frenzy of thought right now."

He stepped close and his sheer presence made her snap her mouth shut.

"In the past forty-eight hours, you've witnessed a kidnapping, unearthed a secret cache of stolen coins, agreed to work with an Interpol agent to solve a serious crime, and have been made to understand that all this may place you in physical danger. Yet this very morning comes a knock on your door and what do you do?"

She pressed her lips together and swallowed.

"Open the door, pretty as you please. No peeking out to see what might be waiting, not even so much as a 'Who is it?' from Miss I-can-take-care-of-myself." Anger burned red in the hollows of his cheeks.

Julia wondered what had fueled the reaction in him. A response to her foolhardiness in perhaps jeopardizing his plan? Or something more personal?

The very prospect made her knees liquefy. She wound her fingers into her lapels and clutched them to her throat. The rubber sole of her slipper skiffed over the hardwood floor when she spun around, placing her back to him. "I knew it was you at the door this morning."

"How?"

Was this where she admitted she only assumed it had been him—because she had been thinking of him? Julia blinked and jerked her head from side to side, as if that would throw the notion clear of her mind and therefore keep it off her lips. She marched forward, her gaze sweeping the open living room for something to distract her.

Cameron followed on her heels, heated persistence in his tone. "How? How did you know it was me outside your door this morning?"

"I—" She grabbed the hairbrush poking up from her purse and began to snag it through her hair. "I just knew, okay?"

"No, it's not okay."

She slashed the brush through a nasty snarl, the pain bringing tears to her eyes. Still, she kept thrashing away at the tangles. She would not let the fear and confusion welling up within her make her lose control.

Cameron used one hand to turn her toward him.

The brush suddenly felt as if it were made of lead. The hand holding it dropped to hang limply at her side. She blinked back the tears of pain and frustration that bathed her eyes.

"Oh, no." He tossed his parka onto the couch and held his arms out to her. "I never meant to—"

Something dark and heavy caught her eye. Cameron was wearing a shoulder holster and gun.

A cold weight sank into the pit of her stomach and she shrank back.

His gaze followed hers to the menacing weapon strapped to his body.

"You're really afraid for me, aren't you?" she whispered, the words crackling in the back of her throat.

"Perfect love casts out fear."

With one look she demanded more of him than his typical evasive answer, even if it was a meaningful Bible verse.

"No, I'm not afraid for you. But I won't take any chances. The Michael Shaughnessy I knew and loved would bring no harm to you." His green eyes grew dark, his jaw taut. "But that's not the man I spoke to on the phone yesterday."

She nodded. Or did her whole rigid body simply sway under the staggering weight of this new information?

"I'm not afraid, Julia, I'm just being cautious."

"Cautious," she echoed. "Does this mean you plan to spend your nights camping in your car outside my house?"

"No."

A quiet whoosh of air escaped her lips. "That's a relief."

"I happened to notice one of your neighbors has a trailer in his drive." He jerked his thumb over his shoulder.

"That's an RV—a recreational vehicle. But what does that have to do with the price of tea in China?"

"I'm an officer of Interpol, my dear, not an economist. But if you want to know why I'm interested in the RV—I was thinking of asking to use it. All of the really suave undercover agents have to ask for cooperation in stakeouts from time to time." He winked.

She hated that wink. It made her feel—it made her feel as if she could actually tolerate the man and his interference. She gritted her teeth and seethed. "Oh, no. No, I'm not putting up with this."

"There's nothing for you to put up with. I'll just go over and ask your neighbor—"

"You wouldn't dare."

His mischievous expression dissolved to a grim demeanor. "I'd dare whatever I must to get my job done, Miss Reed."

She wadded up the nubby flannel of her robe belt. "You really would. You'd really involve that kind-looking, older gentleman—"

"Mr. Wilson. Norman Wilson."

"How did you know that?"

"I know a great many things." A quick wiggle of his eyebrows accentuated the twinkle in his green eyes. "All in the line of duty, of course."

She wet her lips, almost afraid to ask. "What else do you know?"

"I know that my watching over you is only temporary," he assured her, his smile returning. "Just until my near brilliant plan roots out the greedy villain and the fair maiden is safe once more."

"And what if this plan of yours fails to flush out your 'greedy villain'?" She crossed her arms, feeling a bit more confident, a bit more like the good old in-charge Julia.

"Then, my sweet, we go to what we secret agent types like to call—" he leaned forward and gave her a knowing wink as he whispered, "—Plan B."

"'Plan B?' He actually said 'Plan B'?" Craig slammed shut the metal drawer of one of the ancient filing cabinets in the basement storeroom.

89

"A joke, Craig. It was a joke." She stretched out her hand for the files he had pulled. At least, she thought it was a joke.

"He just meant he has more than one contingency." She lightly fingered the white filigree trim on her blue sweater vest, then tugged at the suddenly constrictive collar of her turtleneck. "I, for one, take great comfort in knowing he is thinking of options and alternatives to back up his original plan."

"Well, I, for a slightly more skeptical one, think you can take all the comfort you want. That won't stop me from keeping my eye on the man from Interpol."

"You aren't being very trusting of your fellow man, Craig," she teased, gathering a few more files.

"I'd trust that fellow man a little more if he'd be more forthcoming with us." He stopped to scoop up the last pile of dog-eared folders. "I don't get the man, Julia. For example, what is it he thinks he is going to do with all these inactive volunteer files?"

"I'd like to know that myself." Julia turned and walked through the dimly lit hall. The musty smell of the old building filled her nostrils as she wound her way toward the concrete stairwell. "It isn't as if I haven't gone through these files before. I've spoken with each and every one of these people time and time again, trying to persuade them to help out. Did that make one bit of difference?"

"Nothing you've tried has worked on these cases so far."

"So, what does some untrained upstart like O'Dea expect to accomplish?" She felt her lower lip push out like a five-year-old working up to a good pout. Just who did this man think he was, anyway, elbowing in on her turf?

"And if asking for these weren't enough, did you know he also asked for the shelter's full financial report?"

"What can we do about that, Craig?" She wished she felt as relaxed as she sounded. "Our financial records are a matter of public record. He has as much right to review them as any citizen."

"Yeah, but why?"

Why? Julia had asked herself that question many times since the man with the glimmer in his green eyes had walked through her door. Cameron O'Dea presented quite a puzzle. Quite a puzzle indeed.

The man could just as easily pretend to stay busy around the shelter to serve his purpose. Instead, he chose to dig in and tackle two of her toughest problems—money and manpower. *Fat lot of good his trouble will get him,* she thought, her stomach clenching with guilt at her own ingratitude. But for goodness' sake, his efforts were going to result in nothing but failure. She knew from experience.

She just couldn't figure the Irishman out. Aside from his willingness to pitch in at the shelter, his treatment of her gave her pause. The man, who proclaimed without reservation that Shaughnessy would do his nephew no harm, nevertheless insisted she wear a tracking device. He had once said Shaughnessy would not come after her, yet he planned to stand guard over her personally.

Could the man be lying? Or, at the very least, not be revealing all he knew?

She shuddered, then immediately blamed it on the damp chill of the darkened corridor.

Julia and Craig carted the requested files up two flights of stairs. When they reached the barren but sunbrightened office that Cameron had commandeered for his headquarters, she knocked at the open door with the heel of her shoe.

"Where do ya want these, pal?" she asked.

"Here, let me take those." Cameron leaped up from the wobbling desk and strode the few steps to Julia's side. "Thanks for bringing them up."

He took her files in his arms, then pivoted so Craig could add his.

Craig dumped the files on top of Cameron's load.

Cameron quickly bent his knees to take the added weight. Craig's distrust rose like a wall between them. Hoping to knock a hole in that wall, Cameron thanked him with a smile. "I really appreciate your pitching in, Davis."

"Anytime, O'Dea. Just let me know if I can do anything else for you," Craig muttered as he turned to amble back down the hall to his own office. "Like fetch you some coffee, loan you my laptop, polish your secret agent shoe phone—"

"We don't use the shoe phones anymore, Davis," Cameron called after him. But his good sport routine was lost as Craig Davis strode into his own office and slammed the door. Cameron turned again to Julia and offered her a wink and a wry jest. "We had to stop using those shoe gadgets, you know."

Her blank look said she half-believed his reference to the old TV spy gag.

Playing it up, he leaned over and spoke from the corner of his mouth. "Every time you stepped on a bug while wearing one of them, you ran the risk of speed-dialing an enemy operative."

She laughed. For the first time he could pinpoint, Julia Reed honestly laughed. Not a tight-chested chuckle, or a sardonic cough of a laugh, but a real caught-off-guard-by-humor laugh.

He liked the sound of it. Liked the way her face lit up when it wasn't clouded over with concern. He made a note to find a way to make her laugh again.

But before he could do that, he had a lot of work waiting for him. He navigated the room with his precarious tower of paperwork. Back at his new desk, he paused to survey the pocked, sloping surface, then frowned. With a nudge, he tested the off-kilter desk leg.

It teetered for an instant, then hit the floor with a resounding *whomp*, followed by the squawking of a metal caster scraping tile, and finally a dead thump.

Julia rushed forward, no doubt thinking only she could remedy the situation.

No time like the present, he thought, *to try again to put that smile back on her lovely face.*

He cocked his head to the right and read the names on the tabs of the top files. "What are the odds of convincing A. Abel through—" he narrowed one eye to judge the distance between the desk leg and the floor, "—I'd say, maybe, G. Altman, to put in more volunteer time?"

"I personally maintained that inactive list, Cameron. So I feel I can say without question, you have as much chance of luring them back into the shelter as you do of finding a leprechaun in Cincinnati."

"That good, huh?" he asked, feigning hushed awe in hopes of getting another laugh, a giggle, even a snicker.

"That good," she deadpanned.

"Then the luck of the Irish is on us this day, lass." He refused to be deterred by her bland reaction.

"One thing I have to say about you, O'Dea, you're nothing if not optimistic." She shook her head. "Especially if you think you can get any use at all out of those files."

"Watch and learn."

"I'm watching." She slumped against the door frame.

He skimmed away the top four or five files from the stockpile. "Prepare to be dazzled."

She folded her arms across her chest and shook her head, sending the hair clinging to her shoulders tumbling around her upper arms.

He gave her a quick salute with the selected files, then let the vanilla-colored folders drop.

They hit the floor with a loud slap. He kicked them under the upraised leg with the toe of his hiking boot, and the desk clomped down on the papers.

Cameron tested the stability with a quick knee jab.

No wobble.

He slid the stack in his arms onto the now level desktop and they stayed put.

"Very nice." Julia nodded. "I applaud your Irish ingenuity."

He bowed his head and waved his hand with a flourish to accept her grudging accolade. "And?"

"You're a better man than I am, Cameron O'Dea."

"Now, that goes without saying, doesn't it, lass?" He tucked his chin down and waggled his eyebrows.

She pressed her lips together and frowned.

"Now, about the rest of the files—"

"Too bad you won't get as much use out of the rest of the files as you did out of those." She pointed to the floor.

"That's not a very helpful frame of mind, Miss Reed." He moved around the desk. "Haven't you ever heard of the power of positive thinkin'?"

She raised one finger at him. "Don't tell me about positive thinking, my friend. There are days that I live on that and prayer alone."

He knew that. It was one of the things he found most intriguing about her. He nodded. "I understand, Miss Reed."

"And call me Julia." She dragged the toe of her shoe over the scuff-marked floor. "Please."

"Julia," he echoed so softly it sounded more like a long, low breath than a spoken word.

She looked up at him. "And what is it, Mr. O'Dea, that you hope to accomplish with these files and with our financial information?"

"Cameron." He dropped into the swivel chair behind the

desk. The casters squealed beneath his weight, piercing the quiet.

"Cameron," she complied.

"Rest assured, Julia." He said her name because he liked saying it, liked it enough to know he didn't have any business saying it too often. That meant she should go and he should get to work. "I have a plan."

"Yes, I'm sure you do. However—"

"If you'll excuse me, I need to get going on this right away." He flipped open the first file.

"Get going on what, exactly? Does this have to do with setting a trap for Shaughnessy, or are you just interfering in my shelter to pass the time?"

"Time, sweet Julia, is not something I have in surplus." *Sweet Julia?* He believed the American slang for that would be 'corny.' Still, it had slipped easily off his tongue, and he hardly regretted the use of it—especially when he saw the pink tinge it put on her cheeks.

"Of course," she said. "You do have some serious time constraints. I'm sorry."

"No harm done." He drew in a deep breath. The dank smell of the old building filled his lungs along with a new scent. He'd smelled it before in Julia's home. Vanilla.

He exhaled and ran one hand back through his hair. His fingertips scored his tingling scalp as he forced his mind back to the job he'd promised to undertake. "I know you need to get back to your office, so let me just ask—"

"Yes?" she murmured.

"What's on the agenda for Saint Patrick's Day?"

"What?" Her blue eyes glanced around the room as if seeking the person he was speaking to. "I don't understand. What about Saint Patrick's Day?"

"Well, this is called St. Patrick's Homeless Shelter, isn't it?"

"You know it is."

The snap in her tone made him realize she had run out of patience with him. "So, are you doing anything to tie that in? Are you making use of the holiday to garner publicity, to heighten awareness of your plight, to solicit donations?"

"I—I hadn't—" He could practically see her mentally kicking herself for the oversight. "Well, no, I never made the connection before."

His lips eased into an effortless grin. "Then aren't you lucky to have me here now?"

"I'm beginning to think that luck had nothing to do with it."

$\smile$ 7 $\frown$

"This Saint Patrick's Day? As in a-few-days-from now Saint Patrick's Day?" Julia poked her pencil behind her ear and stuck her clipboard under one arm, staring at Cameron in disbelief.

Three hours ago she'd left him to tackle the work that would have taken the average volunteer three days—with coffee breaks, multiple frustrations, procrastination, and whatnot—to finish. He'd not only completed that task but had had enough time to brew up some wild new fund-raising strategy.

The weatherman had predicted an unseasonably cold snap, and she had committed herself to making sure they had the supplies to handle it. Men had already begun to line up outside the shelter, hoping to be among the lucky ones to find warmth and protection from the night's elements. She had no time, no patience, and a whopping headache.

The last thing she needed right now was for Cameron to come barging into her storeroom to bother her with unrealistic proposals. She shut her eyes and drooped back against a shelf of olive-drab blankets.

"Look, Cameron, I admire your dedication, but it's just not

feasible. You can't hope to pull something together on such short notice."

"I can always hope, Julia. And I can do more than that, I can try."

She doubted if he meant it that way, but Julia heard both challenge and accusation in his words. Did he think she didn't try hard enough? That she wasn't giving his idea fair deliberation before dismissing it?

The hair on the back of her neck stood up. The coarse weave of the surplus blankets grabbed at her sweater vest, scratching all the way through to her skin. She clutched her clipboard tightly to her side.

"It's not as if I've never organized fund-raisers and shelter parties, Cameron. I know they take time and planning. It's not something you can pull out of a hat with a few days' notice." She gritted her teeth against the throbbing pain in her temples. "It simply can't be done."

"If that's a sample of the positive thinking you say you live on, it explains a great deal." Even the hint of humor faded from his rugged features.

She pressed her shoulders to the prickling blankets. "I believe in positive thinking and in positive action."

"But?" he asked, clearly baiting her.

"But," she ground her reply between her back teeth, trying to remain marginally civil, "I also believe in a concept that seems to have gotten lost in that dreamland of your Irish imagination—it's a little thing some people like to call reality."

His green eyes flashed at her reproach.

"If you need a dose of my reality," she went on, despite the burning tightness in her throat, "just look around you. Tonight we may be looking at double capacity. And if that's not troubling enough, every day this cold weather continues, with the increased occupancy it causes, may just be cutting another day off of the amount of time we can afford to keep our doors open."

"Then I'd say your reality is that you need money." He crossed his arms over his chest and anchored his feet on the cement basement floor. "And I'm offering to help you raise that money."

"What good will one simple fund-raising event do at this point?" she countered, her bitterness more for the situation than for the man proposing to help.

"What good did you think you could do when you stopped by the billboard to offer Devin food and shelter?" He gazed at her, unblinking.

She tipped her head back. The pencil behind her ear gouged into the thick roll of one blanket, which scraped the nape of her neck and snared her hair. He had a point. The man always had a point. And it was really beginning to gnaw on her nerves. She sighed out a reluctant concession to his question.

He shifted his hands to his hips, his long fingers flexing against the faded denim. "I understand reality just as well as you do, Julia."

The soothing tone of his deep voice seemed to assuage the awful pain in her head. She relaxed just a bit.

"I also believe," he went on with firm conviction, "in something bigger than our present reality."

She dropped her chin, breathing in the musty smell around them. Her tension began to mount again. "Don't you dare try to turn this into an issue of faith, Cameron O'Dea."

"Everything is an issue of faith, Julia."

His simple proclamation echoed in the small storage space like a gavel rapping out justice in a courtroom.

Of course he was right. If your faith meant anything, then it touched everything. But he had to know how she intended her request. "What I'm talking about, Cameron, is not faith. It's logistics. It's about time constraints and organization—"

"And about getting my nephew home safely to his mother."

"What do you mean?"

"I mean that this could be my chance to bring Michael out of his hiding place."

She clamped her mouth shut.

"What do you propose I do, sweet Julia? Tell Fiona that we must wait until we can form the proper committees, have a dozen planning meetings, confer with the experts?"

The papers on the clipboard crackled as she grew more rigid.

Cameron waved his hand in the air. "Then, perhaps after we've taken it all under advisement, we'll consult our calendars and set a date to do something. Is that what I should tell the woman waiting for her child's return?"

"No." She wet her lips and batted away a stray spiral of hair that tickled her cheek. "No, of course not. But I just don't think you realize, Cameron, what's involved here. I don't see how we can pull it off so soon."

He dropped his hands to his sides. "Then maybe *we* shouldn't try."

She shot her hand out, making her clipboard clatter to the floor. Her palm went flat against the mound of blankets behind her, as if to steady herself in an overplayed show of sarcasm. "You mean you're giving up? Just like that?"

"Who said anything about giving up?" He stepped into the storeroom, filling up its restricted space. "I'm proposing a shift in focus off of what *we* —you and I—can do and onto what God can accomplish."

"Through us," she had to tack on.

"That's not giving up, Julia." He bent to retrieve her clipboard. "It's surrendering."

"Surrendering?" The word dissolved like air-spun sugar on her tongue.

What precious reprieve the very notion brought. To surrender her worldly burden to the Lord, if only for a while. It made her head swim and her heart light just to imagine it.

Then her gaze fell to the accumulation of paperwork layered on the clipboard held before her. The daydream of surrender ended.

She accepted the board and shook back her hair. "We are God's hands on this earth and like it or not, we have our limitations. We can't manipulate time to accomplish the impossible, no matter how noble the goal."

"Look past your prejudices, Julia." He made a movement toward her. "Look beyond what you think you know, and maybe you'll see that my idea is not so impossible after all."

She wanted to believe, wanted to more than she suspected Cameron knew.

He held his hand out. "C'mon, sweet Julia. Won't you surrender your fears and just step out in faith?"

Her fingers ached to reach for his. Her skin actually itched to make the physical connection, symbolic of a new way of dealing with her life and her faith.

She wet her lips.

Cameron made no further urging. He just waited with an open hand.

Her hand curved over the bent silver clip clamping down the mountain of paperwork she still faced.

Could she do this? Did she dare try?

Her foot edged forward ever so slightly. She pulled in a deep breath.

"Julia!" Craig's bellow nearly made her jump out of her skin. "Julia, where are—oh, there you are."

The young man appeared in the doorway behind Cameron. He nudged his glasses back high on his nose and gazed pointedly at Cameron's still outstretched hand. "Sorry to interrupt."

Julia blinked to force the fog from her mind. "That's okay, Craig. What's up?"

"Um, we got the extra bread delivery, but they only came through with half the quantity they promised. The driver has more bread on his truck that he could leave—but he says someone has to call his boss."

"Then call his boss," Cameron said in tone more suited to a phrase such as 'get lost, we're in the middle of something.'

"Julia is the only one who can deal with these people," Craig snapped back. He turned to her. "We really need you right now, Julia. The delivery man won't wait much longer."

"Fine." She gave a crisp nod. "Tell him I'm coming."

Craig returned her curt nod, then spun around and dashed away.

She sealed her lips in a tight line for a moment, breathing slowly, her gaze locked with Cameron's. "It's a lovely philosophy, Cameron. As lovely as a rainbow—and just as faint in substance. Now, if you'll excuse me, I have work to do."

She pushed past him, darting her eyes upward as she added with cold clarity, "The Lord's work."

She left him standing in the storage room, his hand still open—and empty.

"More green."

"More green?" The shelter cook grimaced into the huge stainless steel bowl of cake frosting.

"Have ya any idea what day it is we're commemorating, lad?" Cameron notched up his Irish brogue a bit.

"Yes," the cook replied, his dark eyes glaring up from his pinched, weathered face. "Saint Patrick's Day."

"Saint Patrick—known as the patron saint of—"

"Ireland," the man grumbled.

"Which is known as the *what* isle?"

"Emerald," the man filled in, stirring so hard that the icing made a glopping sound against the bowl.

"Emerald, exactly." Cameron clapped the short, scrawny man on the back. "Deep, beautiful, rich, vibrant, emerald green."

The man scowled and stirred harder.

"This," Cameron pointed into the bowl, "is a sickly, pale, dreary green. It hardly conjures up images of shamrocks and the laughing eyes of little red-haired tots and—"

"More green, it is, then," the cook muttered. He seized a squeeze bottle of black-green liquid and began squirting it in long swirls into the huge bowl.

"So, how are the preparations going?" Julia strode into the kitchen, her head high.

Cameron resisted the urge to gloat. "Smooth as your cook's own cake frosting."

He dipped his finger into the brilliant green concoction and offered a dollop to her.

"No thanks." She wrinkled up her nose.

Cameron shrugged and popped the icing into his mouth. After he gulped down the far-too-sweet topping, he managed to ask, "Still pouting because it looks like this might all happen without Julia Reed's approval or control?"

"I am not pouting." Her full lower lip protruded just enough to contradict her claim. "I'm—"

"Annoyed?"

"Surprised," she finished through a clenched jaw.

"Pleasantly surprised?"

"Of course. You're doing great things for the shelter, Cameron."

He wiped his sticky, taste-testing finger on a damp dishtowel. "I'd wondered if you'd noticed."

"How could I help but notice?" She said it like she had earnestly tried her best to ignore his deeds. "So far you've brought a dozen volunteers back to work, contacted all manner of media to cover your little event, even made some inroads with a corporate sponsor that had refused to renew its contribution to us."

She swiped one finger along the countertop, studied it as though testing for dirt, then folded her arms across her oversized blue sweatshirt. Her proud shoulders slumped a bit as she let out a long sigh.

"What other kind of reaction but pleasant would I have for someone able to accomplish his goals so quickly, so...adequately?" she asked.

"Careful. High praise like that may make me think you actually appreciate what I'm doing."

"I do appreciate it." Her mouth puckered.

"When you say that you look like you've just bitten into something sour, my dear—a grape, perhaps?"

"It's not sour grapes," she insisted. "It's just that—"

"Yes?"

"Well, I've learned the hard way not to get too attached to projects around this place."

Was she referring to him or to the Saint Patrick's Day event?

"Gang-way—hot pans coming through." The cook's assistant came weaving and bobbing by, a huge cake pan held aloft in both hands.

The warm, sweet aroma wafted over them.

"Watch out, Miss Julia, ma'am, this is very hot," the assistant warned as he settled the pan onto the counter beside Julia.

Cameron stepped toward the swinging kitchen door and pushed it open with one hand.

Julia took his silent suggestion that they take their discussion elsewhere and ducked out into the dimly lit hallway.

When the kitchen door whooshed shut, cutting off the sounds and smells of the preparations, Cameron realized he hadn't given Julia much breathing space beyond the door.

She stood, her face upturned just enough so that their gazes connected, less than a foot away from him.

In other circumstances he might have kissed her then. Heaven knew, this was not the first time this week he'd wanted to do just that. He inhaled the faintest scent of vanilla, and it cut him to the quick.

But it was wrong. His obligation was to protect Julia, not pursue a romance with her. His life and circumstances prohibited any kind of involvement right now, and even to imagine they could share more than a working relationship wasn't fair to either of them.

She swirled the thick braid she wore around her fingers, her blue eyes fixed on his face, calm and expectant.

Still, he thought, his heart thudding in his chest, *it's been a long time since I've known a woman like Julia Reed.* Strong yet vulnerable, kind, courageous. Perhaps he never had met such a woman. He hated to think that it could all slip away. Once this issue of the gold was settled, he decided, as he smoothed his palm back over the unruly waves of his hair, perhaps he and Julia could have the chance denied them now.

It would only take a matter of days to wrap up all his unfinished business with work and then—

And then was better left to the future.

"Now." He brought his hands together in a thunderous clap. "What's this about not forming attachments?"

She bowed her head. "I've just found that's the best way to get along sometimes. I mean, something comes along and you really think, 'this is it, this is the thing that's going to work for me'—I mean, work for the shelter."

"What's wrong with that?"

She raised her chin, her eyes tinged with resignation. "Have you ever heard the expression, 'life is what happens when you're making other plans'?"

His lips tugged into a halfhearted smile.

"Well, welcome to my life." She extended her arms out to her sides, then let them drop again. "Our budget should have kept us in the black from one fiscal year to the next, but Cincinnati's recent harsh winter—not to mention last week's cold snap—really depleted our funds."

Cameron nodded in sympathy.

She tossed her braid back over her shoulder. "I can't tell you how many times I've thought a big corporation might come through with a grant or a donation to bridge the gap until the beginning of our new fiscal year. But so far, I've been let down every time."

"And you think my fund-raiser will result in just another letdown?"

"Not for me." Dark tendrils of stray hair danced along her temples as she shook her head. "I've kept my expectations, um, realistic."

"Translation?"

"Translation—even if you have a real whiz-bang party, Cameron, it won't be enough to make the shelter solvent."

"Who says?"

"I say." A biting chuckle followed.

"And what about what God says?" he asked with quiet control.

She held her hand up. "Don't even go there, Cameron. Much as I have to admit you've accomplished near miracles with your own brand of faith, I'm just not ready to embrace it."

"That's the beauty of it, sweet Julia, you don't have to embrace anything." He placed one hand on her shoulder.

The already tight muscles beneath his palm clenched like a fist.

He curved his hand over her upper arm, then slid it down to grasp her chilly fingers. "You have to learn to let go."

Julia wanted to let go. She needed to let go. He saw as much in her shimmering eyes. But she couldn't do it. Not yet.

She looked away.

Much as he longed to stay and talk with her, to help her find a way to let God do the work she could not, he had pressing matters of his own to attend to.

"Don't worry, Julia, it will work out."

She gave a futile huff of a laugh.

"Just as my own trouble will work out. Which reminds me, I promised Fiona I'd swing by her house this afternoon."

Her whole persona softened. "How is Fiona?"

"Weary." He stuffed his hands in his pockets to keep from brushing them through her curls. "Fiona doesn't sleep much these days. But she's in good spirits."

"Good."

He nodded. "And Devin called again last night."

"Really? How many times is that now? Three? Your Michael Shaughnessy is certainly going at this with a very laid-back attitude."

"Yeah, he's about as laid-back as a cougar about to pounce," Cameron muttered, his gaze suddenly drawn to the tracking signal pin he hoped he'd never have to use. "Anyway, Fiona has a tape of the conversation for me to listen to. Said there wasn't anything of use on it, but I want to judge that for myself."

"Oh, judge for yourself, is it?" She copied the lilt of his accent.

She liked doing that, he'd realized, when she was using his own words against him.

She stroked her chin. "Could that be your little way of admitting sometimes we have to take matters into our own earthly hands to make things happen?"

"It could be." He grinned and sent her a teasing wink. "I'm not admitting anything, you understand, but it just could be."

8

M ichael, this has gone on long enough. Just bring Devin home and be done with it."

Cameron heard the tremor in Fiona's voice despite the poor quality of the tape recording. The raw edge of her pain, her need to have her child back, cut through him like no knife or bullet ever could. He shoved at the sleeves of his forest green sweatshirt, pushing them back over his tense forearms.

"If you want Devin home again, Fiona dear, I'm not the one you should be talking to."

Michael's voice grated on Cameron's nerves. He clenched his jaw and forced down the bile rising in the back of his throat so he could listen to the rest of the conversation.

"Tell that brother-in-law of yours to find me gold."

"Michael, please—"

"Mom?"

"Oh, Devin, darlin', are you all right?"

"Sure, Mom, I'm fine. I miss your fine cookin', though. I can't wait to get home to it, and to you."

Fiona's anguished gasp registered clearly through the muffled static on the tape.

"Me and Uncle Mike had southern fried chicken the other night. The both of us were tired of his cookin' so we followed our noses till we found what we wanted. Uncle Mike says he's a natural tracker—too bad he isn't as natural a fisherman!" Devin's laughter punctuated his rambling thoughts. "I don't want you to worry about me, Mom. Remember, it's just like I'm on spring break."

"I wish I could pretend that, sweetheart, but my heart knows better. There's no fooling a mother's heart, you know."

"I know, Mom. Uncle Mike says I have to hang up now. He says to tell Uncle Cam to get moving on the gold. Tell him that, Mom, to get moving."

Get moving. Cameron depressed the off button on Fiona's answering machine recorder. He'd told her to switch on the tape every time she heard from Devin or Michael. They hadn't had any real luck tracing the calls—all made from phone booths in and around the city. This tape and Devin's cryptic messages were his only real leads.

"Get moving," he mumbled. The child's implication, that he had not yet done enough, settled like a boulder on Cameron's chest.

"Now, don't beat yourself up over that, Cameron. You know Michael made Devin say that to play on your conscience, trying to force your hand." Fiona patted his shoulder. "You've got a fine plan all laid out to go into effect tomorrow. If your Saint Patrick's Day notoriety doesn't bring Michael to you, then—"

She could not look at him.

He winced at the unspoken conclusion.

Her chilled fingers wrapped around his hand like a vice. "Well, it just will work, that's all."

Cameron shook his head and the movement brought a stabbing pain to the twisted knot of muscles in his neck. "There has got to be a message in there somewhere."

"Now, Cameron, you've gone over and over this before." She lay back on the couch, her hand covering her eyes as she recounted his previous hypothesis. "You had every local fishing spot scoured after his first call. Nothing."

Nothing. The word fell like a piano hammer on a taut metal wire.

"After the second call, you put the Kentucky officials on alert should they show up at the state park with the moonbow. They haven't shown up."

He sighed.

Fiona stretched her arms over her head and yawned, then brought them down to wind around her waist. "So far, none of your hunches about Devin trying to send us a coded message have proven out."

If that was supposed to make him feel better, it failed to do the job.

"Still, Fiona, I have to think that's my shortcoming, not Devin's. The boy would try to get us any information he could, I just know it." He ground his fist into his palm. "Why can't I figure out what it is?"

"Cameron, I'm the first to admit that Devin is a clever boy— a sheer genius of a child." She jabbed him in the side with her stockinged toe as if to prod him into a better mood.

He obliged her with a blustering chuckle.

"But you must realize that Michael is standing right beside him while he speaks to us. It's possible he wouldn't even try to send a coded signal to us—or that he wouldn't succeed in doing so—under those circumstances."

Cameron wedged his fingers together and tapped his thumbs against one another. "Of course, you're right. But if Devin was trying to get a message to us, I'd hate to think I dismissed it outright. Can I take this tape?"

"Well, I do like having the sound of Devin's voice to listen to." Tears brimmed along her dark lashes. She sniffled.

"He's going to be all right, Fiona."

One tear escaped her eye and tumbled downward to form a trembling bead on her cheek. She didn't wipe it away. "I believe that."

He stood, lengthening the stiff muscles of his legs with great effort. "I guess I'd better *get moving* then."

"Take the tape." She gave a listless wave toward the answering machine.

"Only if you're sure."

She nodded. "Take it."

He flicked the lid open and removed the tiny tape. "I know there is something on this that will help, Fiona. I just know it."

"Then find it, Cameron. Find Devin—and Michael." She sniffled again. "And secret message or no—you still have your wonderful plan to bait Michael with your Saint Patrick's Day activities."

He poked the tape into his jeans pocket. "Will you be coming down to the shelter tomorrow?"

"I don't dare leave the phone." She placed her hand on the receiver.

"That's probably for the best." He snatched up his parka and dragged it on. The warmth seeped into his aching neck and shoulders but did not ease the source of his stress. "If one TV camera or newspaper photographer got you in the picture, it might raise Michael's suspicions."

She managed a watery smile at that. "For what it's worth, I think your plan is already working. It sounds as if Michael is getting more than a wee bit nervous about what you're going to do next."

"Good." Cameron couldn't return her smile as his thoughts focused on the situation and how it might pan out. "Greed and anxiety breed haste and blundering. They'll be Michael's downfall."

"I'll be praying, Cameron."

"You're in my prayers as well." He reached his hand out to grasp the doorknob.

"Oh, and Cameron—"

"Yes?"

"Have a piece of that green cake for me, won't ya?"

He laughed. "Fiona, me darlin', I don't think I've got the stomach for it. In fact, I think that after tomorrow, I won't want to see anything green for a very long time."

She wrinkled up her freckled nose. "Went a wee bit over-board on the decorations, did you?"

He rolled his eyes heavenward. "The whole place looks like it was overrun by a clan of crazed leprechauns. And if I hear one more pitiful imitation of an Irish accent—" He groaned.

"Now there's a fine attitude. An entire holiday intended to celebrate the Irish, and you're creatin' a bellyache about it."

"For sure and I'll have a bellyache if I have to eat that green cake and wash it down with green punch, no less." He pulled the door open and stepped over the threshold. "There's more than one reason I'll be glad when tomorrow is over."

"Top o' the morning to ya on this fine and foggy Saint Patrick's Day in Cincinnati, Ohio. I'm Eric Schultz—make that Sean-Eric McSchultzy for today—and I'll be reporting to you live from Saint Patrick's Homeless Shelter where they are honoring the holiday in a grand old style. But first, Stephanie "O'"Zawicki and George "Mc"Maynard have this morning's lead news stories."

"You're clear." The man with a camera poised on his shoulder gave a thumbs-up sign to the compact, ruddy-faced fellow clutching a microphone.

"You'll be in the next segment, Mr. O'Dea." Eric Schultz,

billed locally as the Wacky Wake Up Weatherman, motioned for Cameron to join him in the glaring white spotlight.

"I want to thank you and your station for giving us this broadcast this morning." He shook the man's hand, surprised at how he towered over the city's favorite funny weathercaster.

"No problem. I have to be somewhere every morning, might as well be here." Eric contorted his face in one of his trademark rubbery expressions. "It's you who did us a favor by letting us know about this, anyway. I mean, how often does something like this come along?"

"Saint Patrick's Day comes once a year, if I'm not mistaken," Cameron said, knowing it wasn't because of the man's stature that the wry comment would go over his head.

"Naw, not that." He waved his hand. "I mean a broadcast opportunity like this. It has it all—great visual, human interest, community appeal, and a real Irish person on a real Irish holiday."

"Actually, this is more of an American holiday—"

"Whatever. The point is, it's going to come off fresh and fun and with just the right touch of tugging at the old heartstrings." He glanced down at the handheld TV monitor to check the progress of the morning news report.

"Well, it certainly is an excellent opportunity for your station to come off looking very altruistic."

"Yeah, and it makes us look like the good guys, too, putting community first and all that stuff."

Cameron's cheek twitched and he nodded. "It doesn't hurt, I suppose, that your main competition is doing a noon report from the shelter, either."

"Won't lie to you, pal, it feels good to get the scoop on 'em." He glanced up at the cameraman, who squatted in front of them and held his hand up. "Now, I'm going to do the weather, then do a teaser—we'll show you and let you say something

Irish—then we'll cut away to a commercial, then come back and do your interview."

Say something Irish? Cameron combed his fingers through his hair. *This had better work,* he thought as he plastered on his best "I'm from the old sod" expression. He hated the idea of making a fool of himself for nothing.

He said a quick prayer that Michael would catch something of the coverage he'd arranged. That it would lure him out of hiding. But he also hoped the massive publicity would generate good will, renewed interest in volunteering, and a positive cash flow for the shelter.

In the week he'd been working in and around the place, he had come to care about the staff, the regulars who depended on the place, and most of all, the lovely shelter director. Knowing he could help their cause made this little green-gilded dog-and-pony show all the more crucial.

"And that's what you can expect for your workday weather."

Eric's spirited summation brought Cameron's attention back to the reporter.

"It's fitting that we're coming to you today from St. Patrick's Homeless Shelter in downtown Cincinnati. And I have with me today a former resident of the Emerald Isle who is going to tell us a bit about the shelter, its needs, and what we can all do to help. Meet Mr. Cameron O'Dea."

Cameron nodded into the dark, bottomless lens trained on his face.

"So, Mr. O'Dea, give us a wee taste of the lilting brogue of the wee folk of old Eire."

Schultz shoved the microphone under Cameron's nose, and suddenly his mind closed up. Unfortunately, his mouth did not have the same problem.

~~ ~~ ~~ ~~ ~~

"Always after me Lucky Charms?" Julia lifted a shamrock-covered paper cup to her lips and sipped at the dregs of lime punch gone flat. "That's the best you could do?"

"He put me on the spot," Cameron grumbled.

"Well, good thing for you, you can think on your feet," she teased, gazing at him from over the rim of her upturned cup. "They teach you that at the secret agent technical institute?"

"I must have been absent the day they lectured on sharing witty banter with wacky weathermen." He scanned the crowd shuffling around the gaily decorated cafeteria.

The late afternoon sun streamed in the barred windows, illuminating the stragglers with a golden glow. Even Julia had to admit that the event had been a huge success.

"You did great. And by the time the last reporter left, you handled yourself like a pro." She followed his line of vision, pretending to be fascinated by the fading flurry of activity. "Let's just hope it works."

"Are you kidding? Look at this place." He swept his hand out. "This shindig has garnered more good publicity than this place has had in years."

The rolled lip of the paper cup scraped against her teeth when her jaw inexplicably tightened. She tossed back the last of the warm but still tart punch.

He tapped his fingers against his own cup as he went on. "The cash contributions have been enormous, not to mention the big corporate check that showed up oh-so-coincidentally with the noon news crew."

Her fingers crushed one side of her cup. "I meant, I hope this works to attract Michael Shaughnessy's attention."

He nodded, his eyes still fixed at some point in the crowd.

"Oh, and by the way, I received a whole packet of informa-

116

tion on Cumberland Falls today."

"Where?"

"Cum-ber-land Falls," she pronounced each syllable as though she were speaking to an inattentive child. "You know, the place in Kentucky—with the moonbow?"

"Oh, right. Right." He nodded. The green shamrock pinned to his collar fluttered with the movement.

"Anyway," she said, trying not to be fascinated with his every motion, "all the brochures are on my desk in my office under the notes you made at the restaurant."

He hummed a noncommittal reply, his gaze on the crowd again.

"I thought you might want to know."

"Yes," he murmured. "Thank you."

"I'm afraid I spilled a little magical Irish fairy dust on them, so they are, unfortunately, invisible to the naked eye."

"Uh-huh."

"But that won't matter too much. You can still find them by looking under the big pink polka-dotted hippopotamus I used for a paperweight."

"That's fine, lass, I will."

"I'd say 'I give up,' but I have a sneaking feeling you'd hear that."

A slow grin broke over his lips, even as he kept his eyes trained on the dwindling party.

She gazed at his striking profile. Standing this close, she was once again aware of how tall and powerful a man Cameron O'Dea was. And yet, he did not abuse either his physical power or his authority. She'd seen him treat everyone with fairness and consideration.

He had a gentle way about him that shone through his jests and his handling of everyone from Fiona to the downtrodden men who shuffled through their doors.

She recalled a Sunday school exercise using 1 Corinthians 13, the "love chapter." They had been instructed to see how well they measured up to the standard of a loving Christian. Julia still did that from time to time, and sadly found the Scripture did not fit her as well as it could. But when she thought of Cameron O'Dea, she could see how he might well measure up to the test.

Love is patient and kind; love is not jealous or boastful; it is not arrogant or rude. Love does not insist on it's own way; it is not irritable or resentful; it does not rejoice in wrong but rejoices in the right.

All more appropriate assessments of Cameron than they were of her. She could see why so many people were drawn to the man with the glimmering Irish eyes. *What an awesome tool of faith that kind of life must be,* she thought.

She, for all her hard work and sacrifice, seemed to be always fighting and flashing, more like a fish on a line than a fisher of men. If only she could let go a little more—maybe not of everything, but at least of the things that had her so hooked that she found herself losing everything to them.

Wasn't her faith big enough to try that? She wanted to believe it was.

Julia sighed and looked again at Cameron's fine Irish face. She smiled at the way his golden hair curled against the collar of his sweater, the one he'd worn the first time she saw him.

He didn't react at all to her scrutiny.

Was he avoiding her because she'd teased him, or genuinely surveying the crowd—perhaps on watch for anything menacing?

He strained to see around a cluster of chattering latecomers.

She strained to see, as well.

Suddenly his expression changed. He squinted hard.

"What? What is it?" Her heart began to pound faster, her breathing grew shallow. "Do you see something?"

"Someone."

"Someone?" she whispered. Her gaze flew to the throng, searching for the face she had seen that evening by the bill-board. "Where? I don't see anything."

"Right—there." He lifted his paper cup, as if making a toast, and called across the room. "Norman Wilson, great to see you could make it."

"Norman Wilson?" She flattened her hand to her chest as her pulse settled back into a steady rhythm "Who is Norman Wilson?"

"Your neighbor."

"My neighbor?" She blinked as if trying to make the jigsaw pieces of information form some kind of picture.

"You know, the one whose RV I'm staying in?"

"What's he doing here?"

"I told him he should come down and volunteer his time. Since he retired, his wife has been complaining about always having him underfoot. He says he isn't ready to just sit and rock, he wants to do something meaningful with his time."

Cameron waved to the gray-haired fellow that Julia now rec-ognized as the man who lived across the street. "He's an ex-fire-fighter, you know."

"No. I didn't," she snapped. Then her thoughts of only moments ago came back to her.

Love is patient and kind...it is not arrogant or rude.

"I mean, no, I didn't realize that." She gave her smiling neighbor a friendly wave.

"I'm not surprised you didn't know much about him—or any of your neighbors. He said they hardly ever see you. I sup-pose it's because you're so wrapped up in this place." He turned to face her, his head bent so that she could hear his soft voice above the din in the cafeteria. "You put in far too many hours here, you know."

"I do what I have to do to keep this place afloat. Nobody else can run it the way I do." Her throat tightened as she heard the defensive whine in her words.

"Maybe you should let someone else try from time to time—or at least let someone help you."

"They'd make more mess than they'd help. I have my own system and it's worked so far. I don't see why I should let any-one—"

Love does not insist on its own way...

She sighed. "Well, maybe, if they had the proper training, I could let someone help—"

"Good. And thanks to me, you can start getting away from this place soon."

"Why?"

"Because your unsalaried work force has blossomed, my dear. Today alone we've gathered a stack of new volunteer applications this thick." There was more than an inch of space between his thumb and forefinger. "Before long they'll hardly even need you around here. You're going to have more free time than you know what to do with. How does that sound?"

Love bears all things, believes all things, hopes all things, endures all things.

"Peachy," she muttered, scowling into her mutilated punch cup. "Just peachy."

~ 9 ~

The crisp March air tingled on the tip of Julia's nose. The clear night sky scattered with thousands of twinkling stars seemed bigger over her quaint Cincinnati suburb than it had over the city. The moon, nearly full, hung so big and glorious against its backdrop that the sight brought a million tiny goosebumps to her skin.

Funny that she had never noticed that phenomenon before.

Cameron placed his hand on her back to guide her along the darkened walkway from the car to the house.

Warmth from his palm permeated her tired muscles. She closed her eyes, exhaled quietly, and let the feeling swirl through her for the first moment of pure relaxation she'd felt in a long time.

The moment proved fleeting. She glanced at the garish yellow beam of the porch light illuminating her front door only a few steps away.

She knew when they reached the door that she would have to say something, to give at least a passing compliment on the day's achievement, before they said good night. She wound her fingers closed over her keys, the tooled metal biting into her flesh. Her shoulders tightened again, and her throat went dry. *What do you say,* she wondered, *to someone who in one week totally reorders your life and even has you questioning the way you live your faith?*

It wasn't that she wasn't grateful. She was. Grateful—and a little blue.

Today, with the big fund-raiser and the ensuing hope of revitalization at the shelter, marked the advent of two things— the lessening of her roll as director and the beginning of the end of her time with Cameron.

His plan for the shelter had brought in enough money, with the help of a sizable corporate donation, to hold St. Patrick's Shelter in good stead until the new fiscal year and their new budget took effect. And he had made a very valid point that she needed to let others do some of the work of running the shelter. Her insistence that she do it all hadn't put them in their economic crunch, but it certainly had contributed by keeping her focused on trivial things while the budget shortfall built to a crisis level.

Besides, she knew that if she didn't use the volunteers who had signed up today, they would slowly drift away and lose interest—as others had before. She had to utilize more people, involve more people, trust more people. That's how Cameron handled things, and she could see the results already.

There was a renewed energy around the shelter now, a greater sense of hope and purpose—and Cameron O'Dea, not Julia Reed, was responsible.

Petty though it might be, the thought that she had not been the one to breathe life back into the shelter saddened and embarrassed her just a bit.

Her shoes scuffed over the concrete steps and onto the small porch.

The heavy footfalls of Cameron's boots followed behind.

Julia wet her lips and pulled at the collar of her black turtle-neck sweater. The golden pin she now wore everywhere caught the light and winked with a soft luster.

Cameron cleared his throat.

Her keys jangled as she relinquished her grip and began to fidget to locate the front door key. She ran the side of her left thumb along its edge, then pivoted on her heel to face him.

"I really have to say thank you, Cameron." *I'm not quite sure how much I mean it, but I have to say it,* she added silently. She threw her shoulders back and extended her right hand to him.

A shower of light from the brass lamp beside her front door poured over his hair and face in a rich, almost liquid-looking amber. His brilliant green eyes softened to muted jade in the yellow glow surrounding them. He took her hand in his.

Her heart stirred just to look at him, to feel his gentle touch. She inhaled the scent of his hair, his parka, the musty smell of the shelter that still clung to him. Her fingers curled around his hand and stayed there, turning the simple gesture into the sug- gestion of something more.

She wondered, as she had begun to do with growing fre- quency during the week, if he ever had similar feelings. Could a man as good and strong and focused as Cameron O'Dea ever care in that way for a woman as stubborn and demanding and, well, flawed as she was?

He clasped both hands over hers. Gold from the porch light glinted in the depths of his beautiful eyes. "What is it you're thanking me for, sweet Julia?"

Sweet Julia. The endearment made her shiver.

"For the fund-raising?" he asked in that deep, lilting tone. "For watching over you? Or…"

His voice trailed off as his gaze dipped down to brush over her waiting mouth. He stepped closer to her.

He's going to kiss me, Julia thought, her pulse quickening to something just short of panic. He was going to lean down, take her face in his hands, and put his lips to hers.

He took her by the shoulders and pulled her closer still.

And I'm going to let him.

Her keys tumbled from her hand with a melodic jingle, then landed with a solid discordant clunk on the concrete. Julia dismissed the keys, the sound, and everything but the man taking her into his arms.

Her chin tipped upward to allow him to move his face over hers.

He cradled her head in one large hand.

Her fingers sank into the warm padding of his thick parka.

He parted his lips, asking with his eyes if he should proceed.

She said yes with a look, then let her lashes flutter down. A tiny quiver started deep inside her stomach and coiled its way upward until she gasped for air.

With that sudden, small intake of breath, Cameron moved his lips over hers.

Brrr-ing.

Chirrrrp.

The phone inside her house and Cameron's cellular phone rang simultaneously.

They jumped apart like two teenagers caught by an irate father.

"I'd better—" He reached for the phone tucked inside his pocket.

"Yeah, me, too." She spun around and turned the doorknob hard enough to strain her wrist before she remembered that the door was still locked.

"O'Dea here," Cameron said, his voice so tense it crackled. She bent to scoop up her keys.

Brrr-ing. Her phone went off again.

She jabbed her key into the lock and cranked it to the right. Her weight fell against the door and it flew open as soon as the bolt released.

Whether it was relief or chagrin that propelled her forward, Julia didn't know. As she staggered to reach the ringing phone, only one thing shone clear in her muddled mind—she had no business kissing a man like Cameron O'Dea.

Cameron was only available to her while he worked to find his nephew. After that he'd be gone. And then what would she have?

This phone call, she decided as she lunged for the receiver, might have just saved her from one very serious broken heart.

She cleared her thoughts to focus on her call and listened intently to every bit of information given her.

As soon as she hung up the phone, she rushed back to the doorway to find Cameron. "That was the night manager at the shelter—"

Cameron placed his finger to his lips to quiet her and continued to listen with intense concentration to the party on the other end of his phone line.

Julia pushed back the heavy curls lying against her neck. She tugged at her shirt sleeve. She tapped the toe of her shoe on the aluminum plate over the threshold.

"Uh-huh." Cameron nodded, shoving one hand back through his glistening hair.

She lifted her eyebrows and widened her eyes at him in an effort to let him know she had important news.

"I see," he said, ignoring her facial expressions. "Yes, I will."

She pretended to look at a nonexistent wristwatch, then moved one finger in a circle to encourage him to wrap it up.

He jammed his hand into his pocket and looked away. "I will. I will. Of course."

She groaned out a 'this-is-important' sigh.

"Don't worry." He held his finger up to her, nodded one more time, then said, "Thank you for calling me personally. Good-bye, Craig."

"Craig?" Julia scrunched her nose up and jabbed a finger into the center of her chest. "My Craig?"

Cameron clicked the cellular phone off and slid it back into his parka pocket. "Yes, my dear, your Craig. He was calling about *your* shelter."

"Oh? My call was from the shelter." She stepped forward and placed her hand on Cameron's arm.

His eyelids lowered halfway as his gaze flickered downward to the spot where her hand lay. He did not shy away, but neither did he return her touch as he had earlier.

Julia wanted to curl her fingers up and pull her hand away, but she resisted calling more attention to her action.

"The night manager called me," she went on, trying to sound as normal as she could when she felt both foolish and frightened. "And said they'd had some trouble."

"I know." His cheeks were taut, his lips straight, his gaze sobering.

"You know?"

"That's why Craig called."

"He must be pretty rattled if he called you. You two aren't exactly fast friends." She swallowed hard. Despite his initial reaction to her uninvited touch, she could not help clutching his arm for strength.

This time he responded in kind, running his hand up her arm until his palm cupped the side of her neck. "They had a break-in at the shelter."

"Yes. That's what I was told. Nothing was taken," she said, filling him in on the report she had just received. "The police are still there, taking statements. They don't think whoever did it is still there. They think someone slipped in during the party

126

and in all the confusion, lay in wait, then rummaged around while the evening meal was being served."

"Craig told me as much. But he also picked up on one tiny detail." He stroked her cheek with his thumb. "When they were asked if anyone saw or heard anything unusual this evening, one staff member reported that he had found a man lurking in the stairwell."

"That's not exactly unusual, Cameron. We routinely chase people out of the nooks and crannies." She turned her face into his tender caress. "I suppose, after a break-in, that would send up a red flag, though."

The pale light of the moon gave a white-gold appearance to the tousled waves of his hair. "Especially if that particular 'cranny lurker' had an Irish accent."

"Shaughnessy," she whispered in a startled whoosh of air.

"I'm going down to the shelter to ask some questions and see if I can determine what, if anything, he took." His fingers tangled delicately through her hair, and his thumb moved from her cheek to whisk across her lower lip.

He still wanted to kiss her. His longing glittered in the dark pools of his eyes.

Julia's body trembled. Her gaze fixed wholly to his. She wanted him to kiss her and yet knew she would be a fool to allow it.

He lowered his head.

She leaned in.

His parka rustled as he shifted his arms.

Julia felt as if her feet weren't anchored on the earth at all. She shut her eyes.

His warmth washed over her as he drew closer still.

She held her breath.

His lips moved over the corner of her mouth, so lightly she scarcely felt their touch. Then suddenly, he murmured something she didn't understand and grazed a quick kiss over her cheek.

He turned and raced down the porch steps. "I'll call when I know something."

She raised her hand in a stunned farewell.

Suddenly he stopped, turned, gave a sad, slow smile, and lifted his own hand. "Good night."

Her teeth sank into her lower lip.

His eyes sparked in that heart-stopping way as he raised his chin and added, "Sweet Julia."

And then he hurried away.

She stood, alone in the halo of yellow light, and watched his broad back disappear down the walk.

An engine growled to a quiet start. A pair of headlights snapped on His car rolled back out of her drive, paused, then sped away.

She pressed her fingertips to the spot where his lips had brushed her face and found the strength to whisper, "Good night, Cameron."

"Stupid. Stupid. Stupid." Cameron struck the side of his steering wheel with each muttered word.

He was stupid ever to have tried to kiss Julia in the first place. Even more stupid because he'd let a phone call interrupt what might have been a defining moment in their potential relationship. And the most stupid of all, when he finally committed himself to take the risk, was that he did not kiss her as she so deserved to be kissed—as he so longed to kiss her.

The subtle scent of her clung to his sweater, drifted up to tickle his nostrils. Suddenly he could all but feel Julia in his embrace again, smell the hint of vanilla on her skin.

"Don't go there, O'Dea," he warned himself through clenched teeth.

Taking his mind off the job, off his one goal, he reminded himself as he drove toward the shelter, had landed him in this mess in the first place.

If he hadn't wanted to steal away for a few minutes alone with Julia, he would have been at the shelter when Michael was. He might well have nabbed the man then and there and now be on his way to rescue Devin, instead of dashing in to try to piece together whatever clues he could gather.

He glided along the expressway as fast as he could, thankful that the downtown rush hour traffic had long gone. *Long gone.* Like Michael. Like his chances of finding Devin and taking him home to Fiona tonight. Gone like the dream that had slipped through his fingers once again—the dream of ending the shame that his forefathers had brought and getting on with his own life.

'Twas the lure of that very thing that had been his downfall. He had been right to steer clear of it all this time, if one week with Julia could make him this careless.

From this moment on, he thought, renewing the vow he had once made, *I will keep my mind and my heart on one track.* He would rid himself of the curse of the stolen gold once and for all and see Devin safely home before he dared to dream of sweet Julia again.

He swerved hard to the right and guided the car into St. Patrick's parking lot, then cut the engine. A familiar figure stepped out from the doorway and approached the car.

Craig popped open the passenger door and slid in before Cameron could voice a protest.

"I don't think you should go in," he said, rubbing one knuckle up his nose to adjust his glasses. "One visit from the cops tonight has already got this place in a stir."

"Relax, no one here knows I'm a cop." Cameron actually chuckled at the cloak-and-dagger routine Craig was trying unsuccessfully to pull off.

"These are street people, O'Dea. You go in and ask a lot of questions and someone will figure it out."

He had a point.

"I can tell you what you need to know, and everything else will still be there tomorrow."

Cameron dropped his key into his parka pocket and reached for the door handle.

"Look, O'Dea, I know there isn't any love lost between us. I don't fully trust you, and you don't think you can fully depend on me."

He didn't argue.

"But this involves Julia," Craig said, his expression as earnest as his tone. "I think we can work together for her sake, don't you?"

Cameron gave a curt nod of agreement.

"Good." He shifted in the seat. Placing his back against the door, he jerked up the collar of his dark jacket. He skulked down low, like a secret informant trying to conceal his identity. "Now, first things first. How's Julia?"

"Shaken, not stirred," Cameron said in his best James Bond imitation.

"Huh?"

He shook his head. "'Twas a joke. Julia is fine, tucked away safely in her little home. Now, tell me what you know."

The sounds of the city, of cars whirring by, the throbbing beat of music swelling then fading, and the occasional siren gave background noise for Craig's assessment.

"I told you most of it already. About how I stayed late to get some work done that I'd neglected in today's chaos." He twined his long arms together over his narrow chest. "And how after I helped serve the evening meal, I went upstairs to the offices and discovered all the doors standing open."

"And that alerted you that something was wrong, since the

protocol is that everyone lock their doors before they leave?"

He shrugged. "Actually, I thought maybe it had been over-looked. I certainly was distracted enough to make that kind of mistake today. And I did notice that you and Julia skipped out in kind of a big hurry."

He pursed his lips as if waiting for some kind of explanation. Cameron would not give him the satisfaction.

"Anyway," he said with a disgruntled sigh. "I didn't really know anything was wrong until I flipped on my light switch."

"That's when you saw that the locks had been forced."

Craig nodded. "Like I told you on the phone, nothing had been touched except the safe—it had been picked, but since we'd had today's donations taken straight to the bank, they didn't get anything."

"Hmm."

"What are you thinking, O'Dea? Is Shaughnessy capable of safe-cracking?"

"If you're asking if he would sink that low, the answer is yes." Cameron rubbed one knuckle against his jaw.

"Does he have the skills?"

A slow smile quirked up the corner of his lips. "Anyone who ever busted into a piggy bank has the skills to open that pathetic old safe of yours, my friend."

"Oh."

"What else can you tell me? Was there nothin' else tampered with? Nothin' disturbed?"

Craig's glasses squeaked softly as he fidgeted with the ear-piece. "Only in Julia's office."

"Julia's office?" That alarmed him. "What about Julia's office?"

"Well, things were rifled through pretty thoroughly there. Papers everywhere, drawers left open, that kind of thing."

His heartbeat drummed in his ears. He fished his car key

out of his pocket. "Why didn't you tell me this before, lad?"

"I didn't think it was important. The police officer who took the report said the intruder was probably just looking for the safe's combination."

"And I've just told you, he wouldn't have needed one." He started the car and yanked it into gear.

"Hey!" Craig braced himself straight-armed against the dash. "What do you think you're doing, O'Dea? Where do you think you're going?"

"Back to Julia's." His tires squealed as he tore towards his destination.

"But I have work at the shelter," Craig protested, hanging on for dear life.

"You want a job to do, then do something useful." He jabbed his chin toward the cellular phone lying between the two bucket seats. "Pick that up and dial Julia's number. You've got to warn her."

"Warn her?" Craig asked, even as he did as he was told. "What should I warn her about?"

"Warn her that she has just become Michael Shaughnessy's next target."

~ 10 ~

Julia's hair crackled with static electricity as she wrenched off her black sweater. The top cascaded into a puddle of cast-off clothing along with the jeans that she had worn today.

Cameron had teased her unmercifully for not wearing green today of all days. She'd explained to him that she'd been so caught up in the logistics of the event that she'd forgotten all about what the day commemorated.

He'd accused her, using a very bad Freudian accent, of choosing to dress in black because she harbored hidden hostilities toward him and his event. When she denied it, he offered to let her borrow one of the dark green laces from his hiking boots, or at least to let him pin a paper shamrock to her collar.

She'd countered that he'd pinned enough on her already.

She reached down to her nightstand and plucked up the tracking device. She slid into an oversized sweatshirt—an eye-popping, kelly green oversized sweatshirt—and tugged on a pair of jogging pants—forest green jogging pants. Humming quietly, she pulled the long hair pressed against her back free from the neckline of her shirt.

With the tracking device clutched in her hand, she padded

barefoot down the hall. As she passed the front door her thoughts went once again to the moment when Cameron had almost kissed her. She took a deep, shaky breath. She could still smell the subtle scent of him, feel the rush of precious anticipation, taste his mouth on hers, even if it only had been for an instant.

She sighed. Foolish, foolish dream. Still, something compelled her to open the door again, to step outside onto the darkened porch where she and Cameron had stood together.

"It's the sky," she murmured.

The sky had drawn her out, she decided, recalling how vividly the stars had glittered overhead. Leaving the front door standing open so she could easily reach the phone if needed, she sat down on the top porch step and gazed upward. The moon looked like a giant wheel of cheese, with just a sliver shaved off one side. It beamed benevolently down upon her.

Julia let out a long, soft breath. She was suddenly filled with an overwhelming sense of gratitude for her many, many blessings. Her mind turned to those less fortunate, and she offered a silent prayer for Devin and Fiona, that they would be together soon, and for the shelter and all who ran it and all who depended on it.

"And for Cameron, dear Father," she whispered. "Watch over him."

Her words were strangled by a painful clutching at her heart. She wanted to pray for so much more, but didn't know if it was right. She was not the type to get on her knees with a wish list, asking that it be filled. "If I were to ask you, Lord, for anything tonight, I suppose it would be for peace."

She shut her eyes tightly and gripped her hands together, the tracking pin biting into her palms.

"Peace," she went on, "for my heart. Peace about my work. Peace about my life. Peace in the knowledge that even though there is no future for me with a man like Cameron O'Dea, it is enough to have known him, to have had him touch my life."

She wet her lips and swallowed, hoping that would take the rasping hoarseness from her words. "Thank you for bringing him into my life, Lord. Thank you for using him to show me so much about myself. And if it breaks my heart a little when he leaves, help me, Lord, to recall all he left behind."

She tilted her head up to take in the gorgeous sky, seeing it this time through a film of tears. Her nose tingled and her chest ached just a bit, but she felt better for having given voice to her feelings. As she fingered the golden pin in her hands, she wondered if Cameron would ever know just how much he meant to her.

"That was lovely, sweet Julia."

She gasped, narrowing her eyes into the darkness. "Cameron?"

No answer came.

A sudden foreboding rippled through her. She leaped up from the step and stretched inside the door to flip on the overhead light.

Whipping around, she called out, "Who's there?"

Again, no answer.

Could she have imagined the soft Irish tones? She placed her hands on her hips. "Whoever you are, show yourself. I'm in no mood to play games."

Nothing.

She rubbed her thumb over the pin in her hand and exhaled noisily. "Great. Now I'm imagining leprechauns lurking about my house in the night."

She turned her back to return inside.

"'Twas no trick of the imagination, Miss Reed."

She spun around to see the leering face of Michael Shaughnessy as he stepped into the yellow circle of light.

"And I am no leprechaun."

"C'mon, Julia, pick up the phone." Craig ground the request through clenched teeth.

"Still no answer?" Cameron maneuvered through the streets of her suburb as fast as he could safely go. He had to get to her. Had to see for himself that she had just stepped out for a walk or into the shower. He had to know that no harm had come to his sweet Julia.

Craig pressed the power button and set down the phone. "She's not going to answer."

"Do me a favor." Cameron turned the wheel hand over hand to maintain control. "There's a small black electronic device on the floor. Pick it up and see that it is switched on."

Craig leaned down and pulled up the receiver, looking it over slowly but not doing as he was told. "This?"

"Yes, yes." The delay grated on his already worn patience. "Turn it on, man!"

Craig complied with a stroke of his thumb. "What does it do?"

"God willing, lad, it won't do anything."

"That's certainly helpful." Craig let it fall into his lap.

Cameron turned down Julia's street, then stomped down on the brake as the headlights of an oncoming car slashed across his windshield. He swerved. The plain white car whizzed by, but he gave it little notice. His gaze stretched farther up the street to the small house with the yellow porch light.

"I should never have left her," he muttered.

"You don't really think she's in danger, do you?" Craig asked.

"Now there's a fine question out of the mouth of someone who is suspicious of everyone who gets close to the lady."

"Not everyone," Craig mumbled.

"Just me."

Craig dropped his head rather than meet Cameron's eyes.

"Hey, what does it mean when a little green light comes on?"

Craig's innocent question made Cameron's blood run cold.

"When? When did it come on?" he demanded. Cameron tried to steal a glance at the device while still keeping Julia's house in sight. They were close enough to pick up Julia's signal in her home, he reminded himself.

"I guess about the time we passed that car," Craig replied.

They would have come into range by then, Cameron thought. *That could actually be a good sign.*

"Gee, now it's gone off and a red light is on."

That was definitely not a good sign. Cameron slowed the car to turn into Julia's drive.

"Pull out the antenna and point it in the direction of that car," Cameron ordered.

Craig fidgeted with the gadget.

"Do it now, man!" He shifted into reverse. If his apprehensions were real, he'd be taking off again—in pursuit of Julia.

Craig whisked the antenna out and pointed it down the street. "It's green again."

The car jerked backward.

"What are you doing?" Craig squawked. "I thought we came here to help Julia."

"We did, and that's what we're doing. The only way we can help her now is to follow her. She's in that car."

"No, she's not." Craig clutched at the armrest on the passenger door as Cameron gunned the motor and the car lurched backward. "She's right there in her driveway."

Cameron braked hard.

Craig's head whipped back against the headrest. "Ow. Where'd you learn to drive? Clown college?"

Cameron stopped in the street and stared at the vision of Julia, her hair ruffled but otherwise looking fine. She ran toward the car.

He rolled down the window. "What happened?"

"Shaughnessy." She gasped for breath. "He was here."

"Did he hurt you?"

"No." She shook her head and gulped down more air. "We struggled. He tried to haul me into his car, but my neighbor, Norman, came out and scared him off."

Cameron smiled. Julia was safe. "Remind me to thank Norman for watching out for you."

"As though you thought he wouldn't." Her blue eyes sparked. "You have a way of catching up everyone you run across in your little schemes and dreams. Norman's inside calling the police right now."

She reached for the handle on the back door.

"What do you think you're doing?"

"We have to go after Shaughnessy." She pressed her hand to the lowered glass of his window. "While I was trying to get away from him, I was able to slip my tracking pin into his pocket."

"You did?" Cameron blinked.

She grinned. "Hey, you aren't the only one who watched old TV spy shows. Just let me hop in and we'll go after him."

"We aren't going anywhere." Cameron circled her wrist with his hand. "This is between Shaughnessy and me. You're not involved."

"If I wasn't before, he just got me involved." She tried to twist her hand from his grasp.

He held firm. "I can't waste time arguing with you about this. You have to stay and talk to the police. I'm going after Michael."

"Norman can talk to the police," she protested.

"Craig?" Cameron craned his neck to speak to the other man while he kept his hand on Julia.

"Yes?"

"Remember when we agreed that the one thing we agree on is protecting Julia?"

"I'm way ahead of you, O'Dea." He popped his door open and got out.

"I will not be treated like a child," Julia called out as Craig came around the front of the car. Her hair whipped across her face as she confronted Cameron. "By either of you."

"If you don't want to be treated like a child, stop behaving like one." Craig took her by the arm.

Cameron released his hold on her.

"I am not—" The momentum as she yanked her hand away threw her back against Craig. She almost—almost—stomped her foot down on his.

Julia swiveled back toward Cameron at the sound of his unabashed laughter. He figured he should take credit for saving Craig's instep.

She glowered.

Cameron tipped his head in farewell and put the car in gear. "Hopefully, I'll have Devin home with his mother and Michael in jail before the night is over. Don't leave Julia alone."

"I won't," Craig said, his arm around the sulking woman.

"Good night, sweet Julia." He could not meet her seething gaze. He sighed and tried not to think of the implications for his heart as he added, "The Lord willing, you'll be well rid of me once and for all come morning."

He did not look back, sorely tempted as he was. He just placed the tracking device on the dash and drove, hoping the precious moments wasted arguing with Julia would not cost him his prey.

"C'mon," he urged the black box. Gritting his teeth, he practically willed the tracking light to change from red to green. "Lead me to Michael."

He uttered a quick prayer for help in his quest, for Devin's safety, for his own ability to handle it all. "And please, Lord, keep Julia in the palm of your hand, for I think she holds my heart in her own."

Surrender. He'd given over his fears and laid his trust in the Lord. There was nothing more to do but watch the tracking device and drive.

The scenes of the suburbs rolled past him. He glanced down a series of dead-end alleys and found them empty. The light stayed as red as the traffic signal over the intersection ahead. He stopped.

"'Tis no use," he muttered. "Michael could be anywhere."

He hammered his fist against the steering wheel. His jaw clenched. Then, heaving out a hot breath, he shut his eyes.

Surrender. The simple message echoed in his head. He smiled and wondered if Julia would ever believe that he, too, struggled with that basic concept every day.

He bowed his head. "Lord, I cannot do this alone. You know where Michael is. Lead and I will follow."

The traffic light turned green. Cameron moved the car forward at a snail's pace. The tracking device stayed red through the intersection and all down that block and the next. Cameron was on the verge of throwing in the towel when another red light caught him off guard.

He punched the brakes hard. The car jolted to a stop. The tracking device spun on the dash, then plummeted to the floor. Cameron reached down to retrieve it, and his hand froze in midair.

Green.

The antenna extended over his shoulder. His quarry, he realized, lay behind him.

A quick glance in the rearview mirror confirmed it as he witnessed a plain white car dart into an alley two blocks back. He immediately turned the car around. Michael no doubt thought to hide out until Cameron had given up. Either that, or his lifelong friend, the man as close to him as his own brother, had just laid a trap for him.

The alley in sight, Cameron turned off the ignition and let the car coast in neutral to a stop along the curb. He paused only a moment to pray for a positive outcome, then to consider the danger that might lie in wait, before getting out. He opened the door with such control it barely registered a sound. He slid out, crouching to use the car for cover from peering eyes—and anything else that might target him from the depths of the dark alley.

He reached under his sweater and put his hand on his gun. Despite the warmth of his body beneath the knit, a cold feeling settled in the pit of his stomach. How could he draw a weapon on Michael? Was the man so corrupt that Cameron had reason to fear deadly force—or to use it?

His fingers curled over his service revolver. Every ounce of his training told him not to walk into this unarmed. Every fiber of his being told him not to go against his friend with a gun drawn. He held his breath. How could Michael have come so far as to take a child hostage, to rough up and try to kidnap an innocent woman?

Cameron alone could fully understand the man's obsession. It was the other side of the coin to his own feelings about the gold, the legend, and family responsibility. Just as he would do anything to return the stolen treasure, Michael would go as far to claim the gold for family, honor, and justice. Knowing this, Cameron drew his weapon and inched out of the car.

From behind the fender, he studied the opening to the alley. He'd noted before that these alleys were all blocked by chain-link fencing. He knew that if Michael had gone in, then he was still there. Moonlight glinted off the chrome bumper, and Cameron glared upward, wishing for clouds.

Wishing is not going to get the job done, he reminded himself. In a burst of speed, he ran from the protection of his car to the side of the building, without crossing the alley opening. Unless Michael was watching from the shadows, he would not have a clue that Cameron was stalking him.

Cameron counted on that advantage, but he did not preclude other situations. He held his gun up, pointing toward the moon that mocked him by making the black barrel gleam like calm water. His heart thudded faster and faster in his chest. He'd faced worse situations tactically but never one with so much personal emotional involvment. What if Devin were in the car? What if Michael tried to use the boy as a shield? What if he had to look deep into the eyes of his childhood friend and pull that trigger?

It ripped away at his being even to imagine it. He begged the Lord silently not to let it come to that, then surrendered it all into his Father's capable hands. Cameron would do what he had to do.

He swallowed hard, drew a deep breath, and entered the alley.

The white car sat at the end of the narrow passage. No movement betrayed the occupants. No sounds. No lights.

Cameron edged along the side of the alley, his back pressed to the damp, cold bricks.

Nothing.

What was Michael waiting for? For Cameron to draw so close he could take him out in one swift ambush?

Every muscle in Cameron's body tensed, ready to pounce. His pulse throbbed in his ears. Moving slowly, he decided, was only making him an easier mark. He had to move and move now. His boots hit the ground with such force that it jarred him to his teeth, but he charged on. Rounding the bumper, he drew a bead on the driver's window.

Empty.

The car was empty. His shoulder slumped as he peered in again, his gaze sweeping the seats and floorboards. The car had been abandoned.

He glanced at the chain-link fence and judged that Michael could have scaled it easily. He sighed and reholstered his gun. The release of all his built-up adrenaline flowed through his body with a tingling force. At least, he reasoned, it wasn't hopeless. He could call in a police unit to impound the car so Michael could not retrieve it. And he could still use the tracking device to zero in on Michael. Since the man was now on foot, that gave Cameron a definite advantage.

He propped one arm against the roof of the car, which put him at just the right angle to see a tell-tale beam of moonlight falling on something golden in the car. He popped open the door and ducked inside.

If he had been a cursing man, he'd have let loose a string of words just then that would have curdled the milk in Mrs. Murphy's cows.

The light of the big, lopsided moon flashed off the gold cast of the tracking pin.

He stuffed the pin in his jeans pocket and turned to shut the door when a draft caused a small piece of paper on the floor to rustle. Curious, Cameron reached inside and withdrew the small notebook page that had been folded in quarters.

His own handwriting glared back at him from the crumpled page.

GOLD. Wait him out. Moonbow. Cumberland Falls, Kentucky. Full moon.

The tension that had been mounting in him since he'd first heard of the break-in finally wrenched free, issuing forth in a deep, resonant belly laugh.

He refolded the paper, obviously pilfered from Julia's desk

tonight, knowing he now had something far better than any Interpol techno-gizmo. Michael Shaughnessy's greed and impatience had made him slip. Cameron now knew exactly where the man would be and when he would be there—and he would be waiting for him.

ᔕ 11 ᔓ

"T op o' the mornin' to ya, Miss Julia Reed. 'Tis a bright fine day for a treasure hunt, wouldn't you be saying?"

Julia gasped at the sight of Cameron O'Dea—dressed in a long-sleeved red T-shirt, the collar's top button casually open, and faded blue jeans—on her doorstep so early in the morning. But unlike the last time he had pulled this stunt, she was happy—no, make that overwhelmingly relieved—to see him. She couldn't really say she felt happy because she knew he had come to say good-bye.

She burrowed her hands into the pockets of her thick, nubby flannel robe. "I guess the tracking device worked?"

He cocked his head. "It did indeed."

"So…?" She crossed her arms, trying to act more confident and brave about this parting than she felt.

"So?" He mimicked her posture, folding his muscular arms over his broad chest. "So, what?"

He wasn't making this easy. She curled her bare toes against the cold floor of the entryway. Part of her wanted to ask him in for coffee, but another part knew that postponing the good-byes would only make them hurt all the more.

She angled her chin up, determined to get this over with. "So, aren't you going to thank me for my quick thinking and swift action in planting the pin on Shaughnessy?"

"Thank you." He bowed his head in a fleeting show of gratitude. "But I can't give you all the credit."

You could, she thought, *if you weren't so stubborn.* She smiled and leaned against the door frame. "Well, of course not. After all, you insisted I wear the device in the first place."

"Actually, I didn't mean I should share the credit." He shifted into a more comfortable stance. "I meant that even your actions, sweet Julia, benefited from the refinement of the Lord's hand."

She blinked at him. "I have no idea what you are talking about."

He shrugged and chuckled under his breath. "I didn't expect you to."

She narrowed her eyes as if bringing him into sharper focus would suddenly help her to comprehend the man. "Maybe it's too early in the morning for this conversation."

"I agree. It's a bit of a complicated story anyway, lass." He brushed his knuckle under her chin. "Best we save it for the trip."

"Trip?" She pulled her face away from his teasing touch. "What trip?"

"Our trip," he said, as if reminding her of a long-planned arrangement between them.

"Our?" She shook her head. "Now you've completely lost me. Didn't you come here this morning to say good-bye?"

"No, sweet Julia. I came here this morning to say 'bon voyage.'"

So that's all it is to you, she thought, a peculiar strangling sensation closing off her throat. *A joke. Another cause for clever repartee.* That's all the more she meant to him. They'd had their

146

fun, helped one another out, and now—*bon voyage.*

She pressed her lips together until they burned. The crisp spring breeze tossed her hair about her shoulders. Her gaze seared into his. Thank goodness he hadn't completed that kiss! She stood on the very porch where just last night he had taken her in his arms. How much more painful his jests would seem had he done so.

"Please, Cameron, won't you come in so we can discuss this?" he said in a poor excuse for an American accent. He stepped forward.

Julia had two choices. She could attempt to bar his way, which would result in an argument and quite a show for her neighbors, or she could let him into her house.

He took another small step.

Now he stood so close she could see the darkened circles beneath his ever-bright green eyes. She could feel the heat from his body and smell the stuffy air from Norman's RV clinging to his clothes and hair.

She threw her shoulders back, but the fight was not in her. She could plainly see that the events of this last week had taken their toll on the indestructible Irishman, and it troubled her. Still, she reasoned, weary or not, he had no right to barge into her home—especially babbling about trips, insinuating she was somehow involved in a scheme she knew nothing about, and trying to turn their farewell into a hearty joke.

His whole cavalier attitude just made her mad. No, hurt, she corrected. No, confused. Confused and unsettled, she decided. And mad.

Her fists knotted tighter.

He motioned toward the door with both hands, as if to encourage her to move back.

Her bare feet did not move an inch on the chilly floor.

"You can let me inside, my dear, or keep me out like a stray dog come a-beggin'." He cocked his head. The softness in his gaze made his green eyes glitter. "It makes no nevermind to me where we talk, but we will talk."

She set her jaw.

He focused those amazing eyes on her and said no more.

She swallowed hard.

The breeze swirled around the two of them as they stood like stone statues on either side of the threshold.

Then Cameron grinned.

Something broke loose in Julia's hardened attitude. That grin, she surmised, and those eyes, should be registered as lethal weapons.

She grudgingly retreated just enough to allow him to slip through the door.

Once he stood inside her home, she gave the front door a Herculean swing, letting its thunderous wham herald her displeasure at having been the one to give in.

"Cameron O'Dea, you are not one bit funny. This...this—situation is not one bit funny. And I deeply resent my emotions being made fodder for your twisted sense of humor."

He looked around himself, then at Julia, his hands open in a gesture of befuddlement. "Excuse me, my dear, but I seem to be missing a piece of the conversation. I came here to talk to you about taking a trip and suddenly find myself attacked as a bad comedian."

"Don't pretend you don't know what I mean." She marched into the living room. "You're not going to blarney your way out of this one, pal. Bon voyage, indeed. And to think I almost kissed you."

"And I you, as I recall." He folded his arms again, the red shirt outlining the taut muscles of his arms and shoulders. "But for the life of me, right now I can't imagine why I thought that was a good idea."

"Oh, ha-ha." She spun on her bare heel and began to pace. Her heart hammered in her chest and her temples throbbed. She knew she was out of line, but the man brought it out in her. He chafed raw nerves with his carefree approach to something she had thought so personal and significant. And then he had the gall to pretend he didn't know why she would take offense.

Well, she wasn't going to let him skate by this time. He had to know that Julia Reed was not a woman to be trifled with and then mocked. She would not let his parting words to her imply that the interest they shared had been one-sided.

Her voice rose as she dared him to keep up the pretense. "You wanted to kiss me, don't deny it."

"I did," he declared softly through a hint of a smile.

"I knew it. You've probably wanted to kiss me for a long time."

"'Tis also true, lass."

"Ah-ha!" What was meant to make her feel smug and superior had much the opposite effect. Cameron's confessions sent a quiet quaking through her body and fueled the aching in her heart. Only her bravado could keep him from seeing as much. She drew in her breath and tilted up her chin. "So, you admit it."

"Yes."

"You wanted to kiss me."

"Yes."

"Despite your 'bon voyage' remark and that crack about not knowing why you ever tried to kiss me in the first place." The momentum of her words seemed to carry her up to him until she stood close enough to jab her finger into his chest. "I'll bet you'd still like to take me in your arms and kiss me till we both go weak in the knees."

"Yes," he admitted softly, leaning down so that his nose

almost touched hers. "I would."

"You would?" She said the words. At least, she felt her lips move. She heard nothing. Saw nothing. Felt—everything.

He was only kissing her to shut her up, Cameron told himself.

He could make no sense of her rantings. He did not have the time to try to unjumble the tangled path of her thought process. And—as Julia had so aptly pointed out herself—he wanted to kiss her.

Not a long and passionate kiss, but rather a quiet, calming kiss. A kiss that promised more than it demanded, comforted and reassured and asked in turn only that she trust him enough to listen to what he had to say.

As their lips drew apart, their eyes locked.

"Well," he said, his voice deep and husky. He pulled the scent of vanilla from her skin into his lungs. "My knees are wobblin', sweet Julia. How about yours?"

"Like Jell-O."

"Then perhaps it would be best if we sat down."

She nodded, the bounty of her dark hair spilling over her slender shoulders and down her straight back.

They moved in silence to the comfortable but worn brown couch.

Julia's surroundings, Cameron noted, like everything else about her, reflected pure practicality and economy. Her furnishings were not as shabby as the conditions in the shelter, but nothing looked new or expensive. She was not one of those directors of a charity who lived in luxury while others went without.

Cameron had to admire that about her. In fact, he had to admire many things about this woman. As she settled herself into the farthest corner of the couch, he thought of the description of the virtuous woman in Proverbs.

She opens her hands to the poor and reaches out to the needy.

The verse rang clearly in his mind. It certainly fit Julia. He tried to recall more of the passage, telling himself he was defining Julia's character, not trying to keep his mind off the kiss and the feelings it inspired.

He watched her tuck her feet beneath her, arranging that raggedy but clean robe of hers over her green sweatpants. *Think,* he told himself as she brushed the stray curls from her soft pink cheek. She kept her eyes averted, and without appearing to know it, swept one fingertip across her lips where only moments ago his own lips had been.

Proverbs, he prodded his memory. How did that verse go? *A good wife who can find? She is far more precious than jewels.*

His gaze went to Julia again. More precious, he found himself thinking, even than gold. Julia, as a wife, would be worth more than any earthly treasure.

Wife? He pressed his back into the overstuffed cushions.

One kiss and his mind had leaped ahead to matrimony. The stress of the week's mayhem had definitely played havoc with his common sense.

He ran one hand back through his hair. He cleared his throat. "I think we've had our wires crossed, Julia. About the trip, that is."

She raised her face and shook her head. "What trip? One minute you're telling me you've captured Shaughnessy and rescued Devin and the next—"

"Hold your horses right there, my dear." He held his hand up. "I never said anything about capturing Shaughnessy or rescuing Devin."

"You said the tracking device had worked," she protested.

"It worked, all right." He kicked his boot up to rest his foot on his knee and leaned back, chuckling. "It lead me straight to an abandoned car."

Her expression fell. "He found it."

151

"And so did I, lying on the front seat pretty as you please."

"Oh, Cameron, I'm so sorry."

He shrugged. "Couldn't be helped, lass."

They sat in silence for a moment. He read in her eyes that she felt somewhat responsible for the delay that may have cost him his objective. He wanted to tell her it was all right, but he knew that he would need her cooperation, and her present sympathetic frame of mind might be just the thing that ensured he got it.

Finally, she sighed and hugged her knees to her chest. "How are you going to find them now?"

He reined in his urge to smile. "With your help, lass. With your help."

"I still don't see why I have to tag along on your search for the pot of gold at the end of a moonbow." Julia wrestled her laden suitcase up the steps and into Norman's RV.

"There is no pot of gold at the end of that moonbow, my dear, but as long as Michael thinks there is, that's where he's going to go. And so must we."

"You." She plopped onto the U-shaped seat behind a small table. "*You* must go. That's your job. I, on the other hand, should stay right here. That's *my* job."

He hefted her suitcase into an overhead storage compartment. "They can spare you at the shelter for a few days."

She sat forward so hard that the entire vehicle swayed. "That's for me to decide, not you."

"Craig said that he's perfectly capable of handling it. He said you're long overdue for some time off, and that with the new influx of volunteers, many of them trained workers coming back, they have ample manpower."

She opened her mouth to counter that claim.

Cameron held up his hand to still her complaint. "Craig also said that he knew all the manpower in the world would not make up for one measure of womanpower, if that woman were you, but that they'd survive without you for a few days."

She slumped back against the autumn-toned floral of the seat cushion. "Yeah, well, Craig says too much."

"We've gone over this and over this, my dear." He sat down on the other end of the horseshoe-shaped seat. "I can't be two places at once, so you have to be where I have to be—and this weekend, I have to be in Cumberland Falls, Kentucky."

"Well, if you're so sure Shaughnessy will be in Kentucky, I don't see why I wouldn't be perfectly safe here in Cincinnati." She felt her lower lip slide out into a pout. She probably looked all of five years old, but she didn't care. She didn't like being told what to do, and she didn't like thinking of leaving her shelter in anyone else's hands.

"Oh, no." Cameron shook his head before his green-eyed gaze latched onto her again. "We've wandered down that winding road already, sweet Julia. I won't risk again thinking Michael is in one place only to have him show up on your doorstep."

"Craig could watch over me, or Norman—that is, assuming I need watching over, which I don't."

"All right, you don't need watching over." He threw his hands up. "I promise the whole time we're gone, I won't watch over you. I won't watch out for you. Darlin', I won't even ask to see your wristwatch."

"And you won't see it—or anything else of mine." She fumbled to button her long-sleeved blouse over her bright yellow T-shirt. "Which leads me to one very important question."

She pulled in a deep breath and made a show of looking around the cramped quarters.

"Not to worry, my dear. The drive will take most of the first day."

"It's the nights that concern me." She fastened another button. "I hope that you don't think that because we've shared one measly little kiss that I would—"

He raised an eyebrow. "I didn't think that kiss was so measly."

"I'm just saying I don't think that this is an appropriate arrangement for two unmarried adults."

"Why, Julia." One corner of his mouth lifted in a rakish smile. His fabulous eyes flashed mischievously. "Are you proposing?"

Any reply she had planned to make slammed into the back of her closed throat. She tried to swallow, to blink, to have any normal reaction at all. Instead, she blurted out a choking cough and gaped at him like a mortified idiot.

"I'll take that as a no." He patted her back lightly.

She continued to stare at him, unsure what to make of his jest or how to pretend it hadn't disturbed her. Had he thought she was such a desperate old maid that she'd try to extort her way into marriage? Julia did not really believe he saw her that way, but she couldn't help but wonder if that was how she had sounded.

Now, more than ever, she wanted out of this situation, out of this close space. She wanted her life back the way it was before she ever looked into those dazzling Irish eyes, before she ever dug up that troublesome gold.

"It's true," she whispered.

"It is?"

"Yes, it's just like Fiona said. Don't you see it?"

He stuck out his neck, as if to get a better view, then wagged his head from side to side. "Forgive me, but no. This entire conversation has veered from one odd topic to the next without time for me to make sense of the route, much less see the sights. What's this about Fiona? And how does it relate to our being unmarried and—"

"The gold," she prompted.

"The—?"

"Don't you remember, Fiona said it was cursed. I thought it was just a colorful turn of a phrase, but now I think she may have meant it." Julia pushed her hair back, tucking it neatly behind each ear. "I mean, one day my life is going along fine, and then I come in contact with that gold and bam!"

She clapped her hands together.

Cameron flinched.

"Suddenly I'm thrown into a world of intrigue and kidnapping and have to leave my shelter unattended."

"It is not unattended."

"And if that weren't enough, here I am against my will, being hauled away by a man I hardly know, who expects me to practically live with him—"

"Oh, I see. You're saying I'm the curse."

"No." She smacked her open hand on the small formica table. It teetered under the sudden impact. "I'm saying, Cameron, that I refuse to share living quarters with a man I am not married to, and since I am not married to you—nor do I want to be—I'm not going to Cumberland Falls, Kentucky."

He let out a long whoosh of air. "All that just to get us right back where we were when you climbed into the RV twenty minutes ago."

"Well, you didn't really expect me to go off with you just like that, did you?" She snapped her fingers. "Have you completely forgotten your morals, Cameron?"

"I haven't forgotten a thing, sweet Julia, including my morals or your reservation at the lodge."

"My what?"

"Reservation. You aren't the only one who can have reservations about this trip, you know." He folded his arms over his chest. "Thanks to the information you arranged for me to

155

receive, I found out that the camping grounds aren't open until April down there. But they have a very nice lodge—and you have a room reserved and waiting."

"What about you?"

"I'm touched by your concern, Julia. I received a special dispensation to park the RV in a secluded staff parking lot to use as a base of operations."

She swung her head to look at her surroundings. "So, we're sitting in spy central?"

"Something like that." He stood, and the size of him seemed to fill up the limited space inside the vehicle. "Your concerns have been answered. Your virtue unchallenged. Spy central is ready to roll. Our bags are already packed—so if you don't mind, you can do the same with your excuses, and we'll be hitting the road."

"The only thing that I want to hit—" She crossed her arms slowly.

His sober expression registered mild shock, but he did not stop her from finishing her sentiment.

"Is my head against a brick wall. Surely that would be more productive and less painful than trying to win an argument with you."

"That's not exactly surrendering your situation to the Lord," he said. "But it is a charming way of accepting my invitation to join me in the land of waterfalls and moonbows."

I understand that you're very busy, Craig. But there are some things we need to go over."

Cameron maintained a firm grip on the steering wheel of the RV. The straight highway stretched out through the already green and grassy rolling hills of Kentucky. Nothing much demanded his attention, making it difficult not to listen in on the one-sided cellular phone conversation between Julia and her assistant back at the shelter.

"For starters, you need to get all the food delivery requisition forms filled out and put on my desk so I can sign them first thing Monday morning. You what?" Her big blue eyes batted in disbelief.

"Well, who signed them?" She puffed out a short huff of air. "You did?"

Her knuckles went white. The phone antenna quivered ever so slightly.

"Well, yes, I know, Craig, that you have the authority to approve requisitions and to order goods, but that's not the way we do things at St. Patrick's." If she'd said it any more sweetly, Cameron thought, it would have made his teeth ache.

He glanced at her from the corner of his eye just as her face flushed a sudden, fervent scarlet.

"What do you mean that's the way we do it now?" Her hand fisted up the hem of her blue-and-white-striped denim blouse, and the tension in her body seemed heightened by the brilliant yellow of the T-shirt underneath. "No, I didn't think that was one bit funny."

Cameron tried to bite down on his own instinct to laugh.

"Yes, I can. I can take a joke. But when it comes to my business and the running of my shelter—" She jerked her head up and nailed Cameron with a no-nonsense glare. "What are you laughing at?"

"Me?" he asked like a kid caught with his hand in the cookie jar.

"Just drive and spare me your commentary."

"What did I say?" he asked, letting his amusement at her emotional spillover bubble up in a soft chuckle.

"Why don't you find a basketball game on the radio and listen to it for a while?" She turned her attention back to the phone.

"Listen, Craig, don't do any more than is absolutely necessary, and when I get back—" Her eyebrows lifted. "No, I'm not questioning your judgment or your competence."

She wriggled in the plush tan bucket seat. "I'm sorry if it came off that way."

She sounded defensive, Cameron noted, not sorry.

"I know basketball is the big attention getter in this part of the country right now, but I much prefer to listen to this thrill-a-minute contest of wills," he told her quietly.

She wrinkled her nose up at him, her expression sour. "Yes, I'm aware that you've been the shelter's assistant director for three full years now, Craig."

"Julia Reed, the team captain, grabs the ball and goes in for a layup," Cameron said.

"Of course." The kindness of her tone had a hard edge. "I know you are extremely qualified to do the job and anything it may entail. Extremely qualified."

"She shoots."

"If you'll recall, I'm the one who hired you."

"She scores."

"No, no, Craig. I did not mean that as a threat."

"Ah, but there is a foul on the play."

Her eyes darted to the side, admonishing his unwelcome interpretation.

"A personal foul, I believe they call it," he went on.

"I didn't mean to imply that because I hired you I could fire you. I can, of course, but I wasn't saying I would."

"The indomitable Reed gets herself deeper and deeper into foul trouble."

"Because it's true, Craig." She put her finger in her left ear, as if that could block out her conscience as well as Cameron's voice. "I do have the ability to hire and fire staff because I'm the director. It's my shelter and I'm just trying to see that it's run right in my absence."

"Sadly, sports fans, Reed doesn't seem able to see that it's time for her to relinquish the ball, to recognize the referee's authority and good intentions, and to *surrender* herself to the bench for a time. She doesn't seem to believe the game can go on without her."

"No, Craig, please don't do that. I do not want to see your resignation on my desk Monday. I can't—" She stole a peek at Cameron.

He caught her at it with a sidelong glance.

She lowered her finger from her ear.

"I can't run the shelter alone." She wet her lips and faced the blurring scenery out the side window. "I need you. Furthermore, I trust you to take care of whatever you see fit to

159

attend to while I'm gone. Do what you think is best."

She gave a long, breathy sigh.

"I know," she went on. "I know. I will. Yes, I will. You, too. Bye."

She clicked off the power button. The antenna fluttered as she pushed it down. She laid the small phone between their two seats.

Cameron cleared his throat.

"Don't you dare start in on me, you self-sure Irish busybody." Hot spots tinged her cheekbones, and her blue eyes flashed as quick as her words, but neither held malice or anger.

Cameron tried to feel indignant over her tongue-lashing, but he just couldn't do it. After all, in one morning Julia had lost control—if only temporarily—over everything she held dear in her life. Someone else was making decisions about the shelter, her safety, and even where and how she spent the next few days. He'd even had the nerve to make her question the way she lived her faith. That could make anyone cranky.

"How much longer until we get to Cumberland Falls?" she asked, wrapping her arms around herself.

"It'll be late afternoon. If you're bored already, you can watch something on the television—Norman has a great stockpile of movies for the VCR. You can microwave some popcorn and relax, and before you know it, we'll be there."

"Television, VCR, microwave? Boy, Norman doesn't believe much in doing without, does he?" She twisted around to gaze into the back of the RV.

The movement sent the fragrance of her hair wafting over him. He drew in the warm scent of vanilla and held it a moment as he contemplated her question.

Doing without. That was more his style, Cameron decided as he exhaled slowly. For years he'd done without a wife or children, without a real home, without the kind of love a woman like Julia could give. His new friend, Norman, had all that and more.

"No." Cameron shrugged to release the tension between his shoulder blades. "Your neighbor is the sort of man who believes in having it all. He told me 'twas something he learned as a firefighter. Putting his life on the line each time the alarms went off gave him a greater appreciation for the things that mattered most to him."

"You put your life on the line in your work as well, don't you?"

He gripped the steering wheel. "But for me the work is a means to an end, a way of reaching my one true goal to redeem my family's honor. To him, the work was the goal—to help others, to save lives."

"You can't tell me your work hasn't helped others. You've saved lives, I'm sure." She laid her hand on his arm.

The softness of her touch made his forearm tense. He shook his head. "Don't you see, Julia? I'm not saying my work isn't important in general, but that it isn't important to me. It hasn't been for many years."

"Really?" She studied him with open curiosity. "Then why don't you change professions? Why have you stayed in a line of work so unfulfilling?"

"Any work I did would have been unfulfilling. Because no work could accomplish the thing I wanted most to accomplish. At least with Interpol I could use the work to further my personal quest."

"The gold," she whispered.

"Yes." He scanned the horizon and the road arching over the next long, sloping hill. "Getting the gold, that's what mattered to me. I thought only that could mend my family and remove the taint of my grandfather's crime."

"The son shall not suffer for the sins of the father," she

reminded him with quiet conviction.

"Ezekiel." He nodded.

"Very good. I'm impressed that you could just identify a verse like that. I wasn't exactly sure where it came from."

He shrugged off her admiration. "I'm no concordance, just a man who has spent most of his adult life living out of hotels with only the company of the Bibles courtesy of the Gideons."

"I'm sure you have your own Bible."

"A Bible, yes, but no bookshelf to put it on. No lamp to read it by. No home or hearth to shelter it or me."

"You don't even have an apartment somewhere?"

A heaviness settled in his chest. He pinpointed some distant speck far, far down the road. "I've had one on and off through the years, but I never wanted the idea of home to become too dear to me. Nothing could take precedence over my goal."

"Doesn't sound like much of a life, Cameron."

"Says the woman whose own home isn't much more than a place to grab a night's sleep between shifts at the homeless shelter," he muttered.

She turned her face down. "Guilty as charged."

"I'm not condemning you, Julia. At least your work has had meaning." The constant vibration of the cumbersome boat of a vehicle made his teeth grind together. "Not like me, throwing it all away after a self-styled ideal."

He shook his head. "After all this time, I've finally found the gold and with it only a hollow victory. My nephew is in danger, separated from his dear mother. The remnants of the only family I have are torn apart, and it's my fault."

"I won't listen to you blame yourself."

"You're right. 'Tis a sad old song." He conjured up a roguish grin for her. "I only meant to say that a man like Norman, he has his priorities straight. He sought to help others, and yet he didn't forget to love and cherish his own family. He has a lovely

162

wife, two grown daughters—the man even has two homes, one of them on wheels."

"You have a lot, too, Cameron."

"Me?" He chuckled with a sad sincerity. "I have a pot of stolen gold waiting for me to return it to Ireland."

"And people who care about you."

He guided the huge vehicle around a larger and even more lumbering truck carrying a wide load. When he eased into the slower lane again, he used the swerve right to study the woman with the earnest blue eyes and careless mass of black curls. He wondered if she counted herself among those who cared for him. And if so, how deeply?

Something unfamiliar throbbed with a dull ache inside his chest. If she didn't care, he decided, as he let his gaze linger on her, he didn't want to know. He wanted to pretend, if only for these few days they had left together, that she could care, that the future could hold more than just the shell of his wasted obsession.

"You've got a great gift for connecting with people, Cameron," she went on.

His thoughts flashed back to how he had connected with this one beautiful woman. Even as he concentrated on maneuvering the RV through traffic, his lips tingled with the memory of their kiss.

"I mean, look at your record just since I've known you." She ticked off on her fingers as she spoke. "There's Norman, who has hardly known you a week, yet he lets you take off in his fifty-thousand-dollar recreational vehicle. Corporations, who wouldn't even take my phone calls, fell over each other to hand you huge checks. All the staff at the shelter like you, and, of course, you have Devin and Fiona. I think even Craig is warming to you."

"Craig is pretty fond of you, as well."

"He's a good friend to me." Her straight white teeth gnawed at her lower lip. "I wish I had been as good a friend to him a moment ago."

"I have a feeling he understands how hard it is for you to be out of—" He paused. "—the loop."

"You were going to say 'out of control,' weren't you?" she asked with no hint of anger in her voice. "You're right. I like being in control of my life, my work. But I will tell you something, if you promise not to gloat too much."

"What's that?" He wondered if she noticed he hadn't agreed to anything.

"I can see some validity to your way of thinking. The farther we get away from the shelter and the more I trust Craig is handling things, the more I can see the benefit of turning my burdens over to the Lord."

"You mean as long as you don't have any other choice in the matter," he translated.

"Was that a gloat?"

"What?"

"That gleamy thing in your eyes." She waggled her fingers in his direction. "That frisky hint of delight in your tone. It reeks of gloating."

"What's the expression—busted?" He raised an eyebrow at her. "But I have to remind you I never promised not to gloat."

She crossed her arms.

"Besides, it wasn't so much of a gloat as it was an observation. I mean, it's pretty easy to embrace a walk of faith when you're being driven down that walk in an RV."

"Busted." She smiled, taking his assessment with an uncharacteristic grace that made Cameron believe she could actually learn to surrender more of herself. "And since there seems to be only one thing I have any say over on this trip—I think I'll go pick out a movie to watch on the VCR. But before I go, I just want to know one thing."

"What's that, my dear?"

She thrust her lip out in an exaggerated pout. "Am I really that transparent?"

"Transparent? You?" He sputtered out a laugh. "With that iron will of yours? Those nerves of steel?"

"Don't forget my heart of gold." She rose from her seat and headed back to rummage through Norman's video tapes, leaving Cameron to consider her words.

A heart of gold. It fit her well and it haunted him. That, he realized with a troubled spirit, was the only gold he should have been seeking on this earth. He wondered if it was too late to begin now.

Julia's eyes stayed fixed on the television screen, but her mind kept going over her conversation with Cameron.

He had sounded like a man ready to walk away from the very job she knew would stand between the two of them, and exploring a relationship together. But even if he did leave his job, he had said nothing that indicated he'd be interested in settling down anywhere, much less Cincinnati. And she could live nowhere else. St. Patrick's shelter was in Cincinnati, and that's where she had to stay. Surrendering her burdens to the Lord was one thing, but walking away from them? She could never do it. A man who loved her would not ask her to do it.

A man who *what*? When did love sneak into the equation? Cameron had given no indication that he was anything more than interested in her—perhaps no more than a simple curiosity about their special chemistry.

Love? The fluffy romantic comedy she'd chosen to watch must have penetrated her consciousness. A short while ago she and Cameron had argued; had been at completely crossed purposes.

They certainly had not acted like two people in love. Oh, sure, she reasoned, they'd bantered, perhaps even flirted a bit, but nothing in their fledgling relationship should give her cause to consider where they would make a home—or if they would make a home—much less start mooning over the "L-word."

She rubbed her fists into her tired eyes to try to clear away the fog of fantasy from her vision. That gave her time to feel the slowing pace of the RV. She saw Cameron's broad shoulders shift as he wheeled the lumbering giant hard to the right.

She grabbed the edge of the table to keep her balance. "Are we there yet?"

"No. We've still got a good hour ahead. But my legs are cramping and I need to stop to stretch a wee bit."

She ducked her head to peer out the window at the massive filling station, souvenir shop, and restaurant sprawling out before them.

Thanks to Cameron's promotional achievement, Julia had received all the back pay owed her plus reimbursement for outstanding expenses incurred for work. In other words, for the first time in many months, she had a few spare dollars in her pocket.

"Good idea," she said, as she made her way through the still-rolling vehicle to the front passenger seat. "I wouldn't mind picking up some silly knickknack for Craig—you know, a memento of the trip."

"You mean peace offering after your argument?" He parked in the lot reserved for RVs and killed the engine.

"You see." She let her hand fall against her leg. "I am transparent to you. You seem to see the hidden motive behind everything I do."

"Not everything," he said, his voice deep and raspy.

The intimate tremor in his tone tripped down Julia's spine. The memory of their brief kiss sprang to mind. Modesty urged her to look away, but she couldn't do it.

They sat there, gazes intertwined, the resonance of the wheels shuddering over the highway still thrumming through their bodies. She wanted to speak—no, she forced herself to admit—she wanted to lean forward and kiss him again. She wanted him to kiss her, and in that kiss to tell her something that would warm her heart—or chill the banked embers of her growing feelings for him.

To avoid that, she dredged through every ridiculous thought in her head, searching for some bit of trivia that would get them talking again.

"Did you enjoy the vid—"

"Do you still have those brochure—"

They both spoke at once, and both in a tight, dry voice, so that when they each feigned a polite laugh and said, "You go ahead," they both had to pause to clear their throats.

"I was just going to ask if you still had those brochures on Cumberland Falls," she said, cringing because it came out sounding like an apology. *Smooth, Julia. He'll never suspect me of making idle chatter because I didn't want to throw myself at him.* She tweaked the top button of her blouse and smiled, stumbling on with her pitiful distraction. "Because I'd really like to have one from you—them—it—one of the brochures, that is. From you. If you still have one to give me—of the brochures."

No wonder I seem transparent to him, she thought with bitter sarcasm. *His presence reduces me to a total simpleton.* A child could read her. She wasn't volume after volume of complicated material, she was a comic book. She winced a smile at him.

Cameron grinned. He did have the decency not to laugh out loud or tease her. But he didn't look her in the eyes when he replied. "I didn't bring the brochures, but we're close enough to the park that I imagine you'll find some information on display inside."

"Oh." She glanced at the complex again. "Okay, then, let's go inside and see what we can find."

⌁ 13 ⌁

ope you don't mind me saying so, but honey, you sure do have yourself one cutie of a husband."

"A—huh? What, ma'am?" Julia blinked at the petite woman in a denim jumpsuit with her white-blonde perm teased out so far from her small face it looked like a fleece-covered football helmet.

"Your husband." The woman lifted the tall soda she had just poured from the self-serve fountain in salute.

Julia followed the line of the offered toast to find Cameron O'Dea leaning against a wall chatting amicably with a black-haired scarecrow of a man in a polyester western-cut jacket and black jeans.

"I met him over at the tourist information center. 'Course at the time I didn't realize he was spoken for, you understand."

The woman gave a little wave.

Cameron responded in kind.

The woman's raised soda popped and fizzed, spewing icy drops onto Julia's hot cheek.

Julia planted her hands on her hips and cocked her head at

him, as if, somehow, she expected him to send her a mental message to explain the situation.

He winked at her.

Her heart skipped.

"I started up a conversation with your man on account of I heard his accent when he asked where tourist brochures might be." She stabbed a red-and-white-striped straw into her hissing drink. Julia moved her gaze from Cameron to sweep their surroundings, in hope of finding a way of excusing herself from an obviously pointless conversation. She supposed she could fake a sudden craving for one of the glistening frankfurters rotating on steel racks in the glass case a few feet away.

The babbling blonde yanked a paper napkin from its holder and snapped it open with a flick of her wrist, sending the aroma of the roasting hot dogs wafting over Julia.

The smell made her stomach lurch. So much for quick evasions, she decided, as the woman began again to speak in a drawling, high-pitched voice.

"Now, don't you get mad at me for sayin' this."

"Get mad?" How could she get mad at her, Julia wondered; she didn't even know her.

"But I sidled right up to your husband on account of I thought he might be, you know, the friendly type." She wriggled her penciled eyebrows. "Like this other fellow I met today with that same darlin' European accent."

Julia felt her forehead crease as she waded through the bizarre conversation to make some semblance of sense out of it. "Year-a-pin accent?" She parroted the woman's exact pronunciation.

"Now, ain't you cute? Your husband said it jest like that, too. Two peas in a pod." She shook her head and not a single blonde hair fluttered. "Well, anyway, my brother Rex and I—Rex is that fellow over there talking to your husband."

The woman waved again.

"He's not my—"

Both Rex and Cameron nodded a greeting.

Julia let her protest drift off with a sigh.

"As I was saying, Rex and I, we're up from Tennessee to visit kin, and it happens that jest outside of Cumberland Falls, we stop to take some pictures and run across this fellow."

The woman churned her straw up and down through the crushed ice of her drink.

The cold, crunching sound grated on Julia's nerves almost as much as the delay in the story. Still, she had to hear the woman out. If she had run into another man with an Irish accent at Cumberland Falls, it could well be Shaughnessy. She couldn't let her agitation keep her from that kind of information.

"And this other fellow—" Julia prompted.

"Now, he was the friendly type. If you know what I mean." She nudged Julia and giggled. "I struck up a conversation with him on account of that's jest the kind of big-hearted gal I am."

Julia pretended to join in her laughter.

"And I was glad I did it, too. That accent gave me fits! What a charmer. Had the most darlin' redheaded kid with him, too."

Devin. Julia jerked her head up, trying to catch Cameron's eye so she could signal him to come over and hear this.

"Did you notice what kind of car they were in?"

"A dark green four-wheel drive jobbie with Ohio plates—I noticed on account of—well, you know, them four-wheel drives ain't cheap, and a gal takes note of a thing like that."

"Did they mention how long they had been in the area or how long they intended to stay? Just curious." She tossed in the afterthought in hope of disguising the interrogation and passing it off as a bad case of nosiness.

"We didn't talk about that." She rolled her straw between her thumb and forefinger.

171

"I don't suppose he told you where they were staying?"

"Nope. I just figured they'd be camping in the park, but he didn't say as much."

"Didn't the fellow, or his kid, say anything?"

"The fellow said plenty. Plenty of nothin'—but it sure sounded pretty." Her thin shoulders rose and fell in a huge sigh. "Said he was comin' into some money and headin' south soon, wanted my number so's he could call. Got the impression that menfolks from that part of the world really took after us southern belle types, you know what I mean?"

"Well, I—" This was going nowhere fast. The woman had clearly encountered Shaughnessy and Devin at Cumberland Falls, proving Cameron's hunch right. Julia doubted she'd learn much more from the enamored blonde.

"Of course, I don't mean your man, honey," the woman quickly corrected. "That is, I thought he might go for my type, which is why I said hello to him."

Julia offered a watery smile and wondered how to gracefully escape.

"But don't you worry about your husband, honeychild. I figured out real quick he wasn't no truck-stop romeo." The blonde gave Julia's elbow a pinch.

If she had thought it would get her out of the conversation, Julia would have confessed that she and Cameron were not married. But she thought it might just prolong her agony if it renewed the blonde's interest in the handsome Irishman.

"You got a good one there, you do, honey." The woman slurped up a long draw of her soda, then smacked her strawberry-colored lips. "Hang on to him with both hands and a leash if you have to."

Julia tucked a stray hair behind her ear. "I hardly think that will be necessary."

"Oh, me neither, doll. I mean, I saw the way he looked at

you when he pointed you out. A man looks at his wife like that, he ain't goin' nowhere."

Julia stilled. "How?" She pivoted to confront the talkative stranger, but the woman had moved on to the chip aisle, her glossy lips moving as she read the nutritional statistics on the back of a bag of pork rinds.

After getting her fondest wish and finding herself spared any more yammering, Julia felt tempted to follow the woman and demand to know more. How did Cameron look at her? What did she mean that Cameron wasn't going anywhere? Did this absolute stranger know something, see something, that Julia's own confusion and clashing feelings kept hidden? She took one step toward the pork-rind-absorbed lady, but a hand on her shoulder held her back.

"Listen, Julia, I've just heard something very interesting," Cameron whispered against her temple.

The movement of his lips against her skin made her freeze. She wondered if she turned around right now if she would see "how he looked at her." She also wondered if she could live with the consequences of such knowledge.

If she saw nothing, it would wound her to the quick, and she would still have to spend the next day and night in the company of this man. If she saw any encouraging emotion shining back at her, it would thrill her to her being, and yet she would still have to say good-bye to him once Shaughnessy was caught. Since she knew Cameron was closer to Shaughnessy now than he ever had been since she'd handed Devin over to the man, she decided she could not risk so much on the observations of a "big-hearted gal" with an overly active appreciation of men.

She drew in the aroma of the roasting frankfurters, held it as long as she could, and used her repulsion to mask any emotion that might show on her face. When she turned, it was with her arms crossed. "And I have a little news flash for you, O'Dea. Did you know that according to a certain woman I just met, we're *married*?"

"A certain woman?" He stroked his chin with one curved finger. "You wouldn't happen to be meaning Imogene, would you? A lovely lass with—"

He cupped his hands to form a set of parentheses in the air. Julia's eyes grew wide.

"Big hair," he concluded with a knowing grin.

She rolled her eyes. "That's the one."

Was it his imagination or did he see jealousy flit through Julia's expression? He reached out to sweep the long spirals of black hair off her shoulder, savoring the sensation of the stray curls winding around his knuckles. "And you say the lass thinks we're joined in wedded bliss?"

"I wonder where she got a crazy idea like that?" She might as well have pointed directly at him.

"I don't know." He smoothed his hand down her upper arm and glanced at the blonde who had flirted so outrageously with him. "She looks like a lass with a pretty healthy imagination."

"Okay, I'll give you that." She shifted to the right so that her face filled his line of vision. "But even if she did make it all up, you didn't have to let her keep believing it."

"You're right, I didn't *have* to." *But maybe I wanted to,* he thought, kneading her arm with his fingertips, gazing at her temper-flushed face and intense blue eyes. Maybe it just felt too good to pretend for only a moment that he belonged to someone—and that someone was Julia.

He glanced over his shoulder, unable to keep his gaze on her too long for fear of revealing too much. "Listen, Julia, I didn't lie to Imogene, but I didn't dissuade her, either. That's the truth. At first it was easier to let her think I was married to you than to fend off her enthusiasm for my accent."

"I can understand that."

"Then, after she started talking about another man with a *year-a-pin* accent, I felt I had to guard any information I could about us."

She stepped close enough to make her faintest whisper heard. "It's Shaughnessy, isn't it?"

"I think it is, yes." He scored his fingers through his hair. "And if there is any chance that he is in this area and could run into that lass again—"

"You didn't want her ranting about the gorgeous country-man of his she ran into," Julia concluded, nodding to show her approval.

Gorgeous? Did Julia really think of him that way? He pursed his lips to tease her about the description, then thought better of it. Embarrassment would only cause her to backpedal, and he didn't want to listen to her deny it or turn it into a joke.

"Yes, it did appear that once the lass thought me married, her interest waned to the point of making me feel almost invisible."

"You? Invisible to a female predatory type?" She shook her head. "That'll be the day."

"Don't go on, sweet Julia, you're making me blush."

"And your false modesty is making me queasy," she shot back. "Or maybe the smell of the greasy food is to blame."

"Has to be the food." He placed his hand on her back to usher her to the RV.

"Why don't you want me to drive this last stretch?" Julia called out from the open side door as she waited for her companion to show his face again.

He'd been on the phone for twenty minutes, and Julia was growing exceedingly restless. She understood his not wanting to talk about something as consequential as finding Devin and Shaughnessy while trying to steer an RV. What she could not understand was his steadfast refusal to let her drive while he made the necessary contacts with local officials.

She surveyed the RV parking lot with its steady stream of comings and goings. The air shimmered from gasoline vapors and engine exhaust, which both gave off a staunch smell. She saw happy campers and busy truckers, but no sign of the green-eyed Irishman.

"You can't hide from me for very long, O'Dea. I know where you live." She pounded the side of Norman's sturdy vehicle for emphasis.

Cameron rounded the bumper of the RV, his cellular phone pressed to his ear.

"Aren't you off that phone yet?" She groaned and looked heavenward.

He crimped his brow down and fine lines fanned out from his eyes, narrowed in concentration.

He was gorgeous. Imogene couldn't have been the only woman in his life to think so. In fact, Julia admitted, the cheery blonde hadn't even been the only woman today to find Cameron compellingly attractive. Julia found him so every day.

She swallowed hard and let go of the once-fresh fabric of her blouse, now wrinkled by the dampness of her palm. This was silly, she thought, to have to stand here and wait—and watch Cameron—when she could be making good use of her skills and time.

"Just let me drive, Cameron, and you can sit in the passenger seat and talk to your heart's content."

He mouthed an unnecessarily exaggerated "No" in answer to her query.

She harumphed at his refusal. Knowing they were so close to the kidnapper and knowing that her feelings for Cameron would have to go unresolved until Devin was safe and Shaughnessy captured made her all the more anxious to get underway.

"Please," she mouthed back at him.

He shook his head so hard a lock of golden hair fell over one eye.

"Oh, c'mon." She waved away his cynical expression. "I can do it. What makes you think I can't do it?"

"Uh-huh," he said into the phone. "That's right."

"Just give me the keys." She thrust out her hand, motioning for him to fork over the keys. "You can trust me."

"I said no." He slapped at her eager, grasping fingers. "No, not you, Officer. I have a rather rowdy troublemaker on my hands and I—"

She crinkled her nose up at him.

"What's that? Why, no, I don't think I'll need to make use of your jail, but I won't rule it out."

She stuck her tongue out at him. "Very funny."

He arched an eyebrow in response, making the haphazard strand of hair fall farther and snag on his dark eyelashes. "Actually, now that I consider it, Officer, placing her in your custody might just be the safest thing I can do for her."

She bit her lower lip and flicked at the wayward lock of hair tumbling over his eye, but struck the bridge of his nose instead.

"And for myself," he added, rubbing between his eyes with the back of his hand.

"Sorry," she whispered. She tugged at the collar of her T-shirt. "Maybe I can kiss it and make it better."

Cameron looked up sharply. "On second thought, Officer, she's such a desperate and unpredictable sort that I'd best keep her under my watchful eye at all times. But I thank you for the asking." He held his hand up to keep her from further comment while he finished his conversation.

"Oh, wait!" Julia leaped down from her perch over him on the steps. "I just remembered that your gal-pal Imogene said that Shaughnessy was driving a blue four-wheel drive something-or-another."

"Yes," he said. "That should be adequate coverage."

She waved both hands in the air. "Tell him about the four-wheel drive. Dark blue."

"Yes, I have notified the parks department and state police, but since he's taken the child across state lines, I also had to contact the FBI."

"The FBI?" Julia echoed in hushed awe. She wet her lips and gazed up at Cameron. "They need to know about the four-wheel drive, too."

Cameron put his finger to her lips to quiet her.

She contemplated biting his finger, but then decided against it. She'd already whacked him across the nose. That was more than enough violence for her taste.

"Thank you, Officer." He nodded. "I'll be very careful. Thank you."

He lowered the phone and clicked off the power.

"Why didn't you tell him about the four-wheel drive vehicle?" She planted her hands on her hips. "Honestly, Cameron, were you so busy tuning out my request to drive that you didn't hear anything else I said?"

"I do recall hearing something about a kiss to make it better." He inched forward.

"Talk about selective hearing," Julia muttered. "What about the dark blue—"

"Green."

"What?"

"The vehicle—'tis green."

A tiny gasp filled her throat as she flattened her palm to her chest. "That's right. She did say green. But how did you know?"

"I've known what Michael was driving since before we left this morning."

"You have?"

"Make, model, license plate number—and how much he paid for the rental." He slid the antenna into its socket.

"But—why didn't you tell me that?"

"Because, sweet Julia—" He touched his finger to the tip of her nose. "—you are not the officer on the case."

"But I could have been watching for it as we drove. I might have spotted it and broken the case wide open. I—"

"Am newly embracing the spiritual concept of surrender," he reminded her. "You no longer have to be the one who saves the day, who rushes to the rescue, who shoulders all the responsibilities, who 'cracks the case wide open.' Isn't that right, Julia?"

She snapped her mouth shut.

"I thought so."

"I bet there are a lot of other things you've been keeping from me as well, aren't there?"

"Nothing that you need to know, Julia. I wouldn't withhold anything from you if I thought you really needed it."

"Except the keys to the RV," she mumbled.

"And why would you be needing those?"

"So I can drive us the rest of the way to the state park," she sing-songed right back in his face.

"Surrender, Julia." He met her gaze nose to nose. "You'd be amazed at how gracious the Lord is when you finally do."

"I know the Lord is gracious, O'Dea." She pulled away from him.

He smiled at her.

"You, on the other hand," she said as she whirled around and climbed inside the RV, "are a—a man."

She slammed the door and dropped into her seat, thankful

this little excursion, and the emotional roller coaster Cameron O'Dea inspired in her heart, would soon be over.

～ 14 ～

Dupont Lodge," Julia murmured as the RV rolled down a narrow road through the park. "Hey, isn't that where I get off?"

"That's where you'll be staying, yes." He guided the massive vehicle along a low, sloping curve.

"Should I have leaped out the window or something? I mean, I don't want to inconvenience you by making you stop, or even slow down, just so I can get to my room."

The terse clip of her remark plucked at Cameron's taut nerves. He was so close to nabbing Michael that he could all but smell it. He didn't have the time or the patience to trade quips even with Julia, and her increasingly testy attitude only cranked up the vise-like pressure of his stress.

"Much as I would have loved to have sent you sailing right out on your—way, it would not have been a very good idea." He eyed the road with the heightened awareness of a bloodhound sniffing out a trail. "We have no idea where Michael and Devin are. They could be staying at that very lodge."

"You mean you don't know? I thought you'd have had the whole place overrun with informants, and by now you'd have every niggling detail available except maybe whether Shaughnessy prefers paper or plastic."

"Plastic."

"What?"

"He recycles."

She rolled her eyes. "My point is—"

"Your point, sweet Julia, is well taken. I do have people looking out for them in the park and in surrounding areas. At my last contact—at our last rest stop—no one had seen anyone fitting Michael or Devin's description. No sighting had been made of their vehicle. Satisfied?"

"Look, Cameron. I apologize if I snapped at you, but it's not easy for me just to ride along and not know what's happening, not to have a part to play."

Spotting a secluded road with a sign posted reading, "No Unauthorized Vehicles," Cameron turned onto it.

Limbs from low hanging trees whacked at the top and sides of the RV as the tires bounced and jolted over every dip, rock, and pothole in the road.

He could feel Julia's gaze on his profile. He knew she expected some kind of response, but he had none to give. He'd only asked her a dozen times to surrender even a little of her need to control the circumstances. He did not have it in him to ask again.

"I know you have your reasons, your motives, your goal," she said, seizing on his silence. "But since you dragged me into this—and you did drag me; you can't say I haven't fought it."

He tipped his head to one side to concede that.

"I just think it's only fair that you be a little more forthcoming. I'm not asking you to reveal any big secrets. I'm just saying that—" She wrung her hands together and let out an exasperated huff of air. "—Cameron, I just can't stand to be left in the dark with you."

A stone struck the underside of the RV with a resounding thunk.

"Well," he said after a moment to let her choice of words settle in. "You certainly know how to bruise a man's ego, I can say that for you, sweet Julia."

"I didn't mean it that way. That is, I didn't not mean it that way, either—not that I wouldn't want to be in the dark, but that I don't—"

He guided the RV into a secluded spot reserved for park personnel and cut the engine.

"I know what you meant, Julia." He held up his hand to quiet her. "And you make a reasonable point."

"I do?" She blinked, flicked back her hair, tugged at her shirt collar, and then blinked again. "I mean, yes, I do."

She cleared her throat. Her eyes narrowed to slits. "Now, just what point was that?"

"I did drag you along. And you probably deserve to know a bit more than I have elected to share with you."

"So." She clapped her hands, then rubbed them together. "You're going to clue me in on the whole game plan."

He frowned.

"You're going to brief me on key factors in order to find the ways in which I can be of the most help."

He laughed.

"You're going to ramble off a few evasive comments, wedge in some witty asides, pepper it with 'sweet Julias' and Irish quaintisms, and on the whole leave me with no more hard evidence or information than I had before."

He stroked his chin and hummed as if he were seriously considering that line of action.

She glowered at him.

He squirmed from the driver's seat to avoid her scrutiny. "I've scheduled a meeting with an FBI agent and a park official.

183

They should arrive in the next fifteen minutes or so."

The RV swayed slightly under the weight of his movements to collect his phone, his notes, and his composure. Finally, he pushed open the side door and climbed outside. Even as he inhaled the humid air, rich with the smell of the earth and the blossoming foliage, his shoulders tensed. Behind him he could hear Julia shifting about in the RV. Then he felt her standing in the doorway directly behind him.

"Can't I at least ask you a few questions?" she demanded.

"You can ask." He tried to shrug, but the bonds of his clenched muscles would not allow more than a jerking shirk.

"Okay." She remained in the doorway, standing over him.

He could feel the heat of her body, hear the rustling of her cotton shirt each time she snatched at the hem. He smelled her vanilla-scented skin. Her every breath pricked at his alerted senses.

"I'll ask," she said. "For starters, why can't you just let the FBI pick up Shaughnessy? Why did you have to come?"

Cameron's mind flashed back to that moment when he had entered the alley, his gun drawn. He knew a stranger, a well-trained agent of the law, would not hesitate, as he had, to use deadly force against a kidnapper. He exhaled a hard puff of air. "Because it's personal, Julia. A family matter as well as a criminal act."

"You think you can still reason with Shaughnessy, don't you?"

"He's been like a brother to me. Like an uncle to Devin. 'Tis the gold that's blinded him to his own better qualities. But maybe I can still reach him."

"And what if you can't?"

He searched out a spot deep in the thick tangle of trees and underbrush, his gaze fixing so hard on the distance that his eyes ached. "Then I'll do what I must."

"That's why you didn't want me to stay in Cincinnati, even with an armed guard. Because you didn't want anyone else to encounter Shaughnessy. You have to do it yourself."

He nodded, not shifting his focus.

"I understand."

"You do?" He twisted his head until his chin brushed against the fabric of his red shirt.

"You doubt that the queen of control doesn't understand the need to handle things your way, in your time, on your terms because you see them as your responsibility?" Laughter and disbelief layered the rhetorical question.

He chuckled.

"Where's your sweet surrender now, Cameron?" she asked quietly, no trace of mockery in her tone.

"It's there, Julia," he whispered. "In more ways than you can know. It's there."

"Cameron?"

"What?"

"There's one more thing I have to know."

"What's that?"

"Were you using me as bait to lure Shaughnessy out of hiding?"

The wind hurled dust and bits of dried leaves around the open space where he had parked. The late afternoon sun hung low, a blaze of orange and pink above the hilltops plush with trees. Cameron shaded his eyes with one hand. "I knew Michael would never hurt you, Julia."

"There you go again, avoiding the question." She slapped her hand to her blue-jeaned thigh. "It's a fairly straightforward question, Cameron. Just give me a straightforward answer. Did you use me as bait—yes or no?"

"Yes." He blew out a long, unburdening sigh. "Or no."

She groaned through clenched teeth.

An easy laughter rolled from his constricted chest. He

185

turned on the heel of his boot to face her. "It's just not a yes or no proposition, Julia. If you're asking did I know that Michael would make the connection between you and the gold? Yes. Yes, I did. Maybe in that way I used you as bait."

Julia leaned her hip against the door frame, her arms crossed over her chest. She dropped her chin, caught him in an expectant gaze, and waited.

"If you're asking did I know that he would come for you? Then, no. I would never have put you in that kind of danger." The grass under his boots swished as he shifted his weight. "But from the moment you told me about your meeting with Michael and the fact that he had taken down your license plate number, you became wrapped up in the conflict."

"My license plate?"

"That's how he found your house, Julia."

"He could do that?"

"Anyone could do that."

"That gives me the creeps, thinking a man like Shaughnessy could just look into my private records like that."

"I guess this would be a good time for a little confession of my own," Cameron said.

"Oh?"

"Before I walked into St. Patrick's Homeless Shelter a bit more than a week ago, I pulled together a file on you. Medical, work, personal. I know more about your dirty laundry than your own dry cleaner, which, in case you don't believe me, is Speed Clean on the corner of—"

"I get it." She held her hand up.

"Are you angry with me, sweet Julia?"

She cocked her head and blinked.

"You have to recall that I knew you'd taken the gold almost immediately," he said. "I had to know what manner of person I was dealing with."

Her cheeks glowed a charming shade of pink. She nodded. "I understand. I just—well, I cringe to think what you might have discovered about me."

His heart warmed to know she would not hold the necessity of his work against him. He reached out to place his hand along her jaw, his fingers caressing her hot cheek. "Sweet, sweet Julia. I learned more about you the day I looked into your eyes than I ever did from a piece of paper."

Not far behind them the rumble of a car jostling over the rugged terrain drew their attention.

"That's probably the men I'm meeting with, but just in case, why don't you slip back inside?" He cupped his hand under her chin, then slid his palm down her neck. "After the meeting we'll know if it's safe for you to go to the lodge, then you can get some dinner. And later, when it's nice and dark—"

She wet her lips. "Yes?"

"We'll go see the moonbow."

The moonbow. The very word evoked something compelling and awe inspiring.

Julia smiled as she zipped up her red jacket and grabbed her room key. She stole one last look in the mirror to make sure she didn't have any of the evening's delicious dinner stuck between her front teeth, then whisked back her hair and hurried out. Her sad little loafers slapped a happy cadence on the floor as she went on her way.

Despite her misgivings about coming, she had to admit she couldn't wait to hike the trail and see what wonders the Lord had created with the mix of moon and mist. In fact, everywhere that Julia looked in the natural setting of the state park, she saw the evidence of God's majesty.

And it didn't hurt that Cameron would be at her side to

view the wonder of the moonbow. She rushed down the stair-case of the lodge. After dinner in her room—a safety precau-tion—Julia couldn't wait for some fresh air. She and Cameron had arranged to meet a half hour before the prime viewing time.

She practically skipped across the main lobby to the adjoin-ing sitting room, her attention going to the fireplace dominating the scene.

She had pictured coming downstairs in the beautiful lodge to find Cameron leaning with one elbow on the mantle, beam-ing that thousand-watt grin at her. From somewhere in the lodge, music from a grand piano would swell and fill the air around them. He'd wear one of those sweaters, made of the fine Irish wool that set off the healthy coloring of his face. His hair, tousled just enough to hint at casual masculine disarray, would gleam golden in the firelight. And his eyes—those eyes that had first drawn her to him, those dazzling green Irish eyes that could win the heart of any woman in the room—would shine only for her.

She had to laugh at her own romanticized fantasy. Still, her pulse did pick up a beat. Her breathing grew quick and shal-low. She bit her lower lip in anticipation. She tossed back her hair, squared her shoulders, and walked into the sitting room.

Empty.

That's what she found, an empty room—save the huge chair turned away from the door and the more typical furnishings. No fire. No music. No Cameron.

He'd never been late before. Not that she'd known him so very long, but from what she did know, he was not the type to arrive fashionably late. Something, she decided with a haste bordering on panic, must have happened to him.

A dozen scenarios darted through her thoughts. Could he have gotten a tip on Shaughnessy's whereabouts and gone after him? Surely he would have left a note. Could he have merely made this date to keep her busy while he went ahead to stake out the moonbow? Not if he wanted to survive the trip home with her, he wouldn't. Her mind honed in on a third, more terrifying possibility.

Shaughnessy had gotten to Cameron.

What else could it be? She balled the cuffs of her jacket in her fists. Her heart hammered in her chest, her throat, her temples.

If something had happened to Cameron, Julia realized, she was on her own. She had to make a plan, she had to find help, she had to—

"Surprise."

Julia gurgled a sharp gasp. She swung around, ready to push Shaughnessy aside and run. From the corner of her eye, she caught a flicker of movement from the big chair. Her alarm flamed higher. She closed her eyes and shoved hard. The shuffling of feet, paper crinkling, and a loud thump answered her maneuver.

"Whoa." Cameron's strong hands clasped her arms. "Julia? What's wrong? Where are you going?"

She opened her eyes slowly to peer up into the eyes that could see right into her heart.

"Cameron," she murmured.

"Are you okay?" He bent at the knees to level his gaze with hers.

She wet her lips and nodded, a little embarrassed at her overreaction to the situation. That's when she noticed the man in a blue jacket and jeans lurking just over her shoulder. She flinched as she twisted to glance back.

At the same moment, Cameron nodded a greeting to the man.

"You have this man shadowing me." She put her hand on Cameron's green parka.

"It's nighttime, Julia. You don't cast a shadow."

"You know what I mean."

"I know," he said. "We have to get going if we expect to see the moonbow."

"One day, you're going to accidentally give me a straight answer, and then what will you do?"

He arched an eyebrow. "Pick you up from a dead faint?"

She rolled her eyes and laughed.

"But before we go, I have a little gift for you." He bent down to snatch up the shiny paper shopping bag tipped over by his feet.

"Oh, no." She waved her hands and pulled her shoulders back. "No, no, I can't accept any presents."

He thrust the bag toward her. "Well, you had better take this one, lass, if you count on going with me on the moonbow trail tonight."

She cocked her head at him. The bag rustled as she reached inside to pull out a square box with both hands. "What is this?"

"Open it and see."

She pulled at the top of the box, and it flipped open and tumbled to the floor.

"Hiking boots."

"Hmm." He dragged one knuckle down his jaw. "I've heard that when a person repeats what they've received, it means they don't like it."

"No, no." She shook her head so fast that a trembling curl dropped across the bridge of her nose. "I like them. I—like them."

"You need them." He tapped the toe of his own hiking boot against the ratty edge of her loafer. "You can't go hiking a trail in the dark on a damp spring evening in those."

"It's very thoughtful of you, Cameron." She meant that. "But I have to insist that I repay you for these."

"You can repay me by wearing them. That way I won't worry so much." He took the box and lowered himself to his knees as he began to help her into the new shoes.

"You worry about me?"

He slipped her loafer off, his hands warm and gentle. He didn't answer her question.

She watched him help her fit into her new shoes. The sight made her feel cherished and special and—watched.

The man in the blue jacket folded his hands in front of him, anchoring his feet shoulder width apart.

"If you really worry about me, then you'd worry about my feelings as well as my feet, right?"

"In theory," he muttered.

"Then how about this—I'll accept the shoes if you'll accept my feelings."

The new laces hissed as he pulled them taut.

"Take my proposition or take these hiking shoes off." *Cameron O'Dea isn't the only one capable of the big bluff,* Julia thought. "What will it be?"

He tied the laces into a stiff knot.

"What is it you want, sweet Julia?"

"To go out on this hike with you alone." She glanced at the man meant to play bodyguard to her. "All alone."

⤳ 15 ⤲

Thank you for giving my bodyguard a few hours off. I think we're old enough to go on a moonlight hike without a chaperone." Julia's new hiking boots crushed a twig on the well-traveled trail.

The brittle snap rang in Cameron's ears. Every whoosh of a branch, every tripping scuttle of a loose stone, every voice from some other hiker on the path registered, setting his teeth on edge. "Much as I appreciate the privacy your request granted us, lass, I can't say I'm entirely comfortable with these circumstances."

"You mean because of Shaughnessy?"

He took one long stride and came up directly behind her. Using his sheer physical advantage, he pulled her back, pressing their bodies together so that he could whisper in her ear unheard by others. "Don't utter that name again, lass. Not until it's over and done with. You never know who might hear. Do you understand?"

She nodded. Her thick hair rustled, the fine curls tickling his cheek and nose. He felt her tense muscles strain against him.

He kept his voice a gravel-throated growl. "Are you afraid?"

He heard her gulp down a swallow. Felt the tremble of her lips as she wet them. "A little."

"That's good," he murmured against her temple. "A little afraid makes for a lot of caution. Before this little family adventure branched out to include you, 'twas sport—a game of cat and mouse. Have caution, sweet Julia, this is a game no more."

"Are you afraid?" she asked as they continued to walk again, still so close they could hear each breath before a word was spoken.

"I would be," he confessed. "The whole affair has escalated so far from what it was even a week ago. What with Devin taken and now the FBI involved. I don't wish any harm to come to my childhood friend. I also hope that this greed doesn't cause him to harm anyone."

"But you don't fear it?"

"I've left it in the Lord's hands."

They could hear the waterfalls now, the powerful rush of water, the oohs and ahhs of the people ahead of them on the trail.

They moved on in silence until they came to the spot set aside for optimum viewing of the impressive phenomenon. Mist from the falls caught the moonlight, forming a pure white rainbow that spanned the churning waters.

"'Tis even more lovely than I'd imagined." Cameron stepped behind Julia again. He wrapped his arms around her and rested his chin against her hair as they admired the unique view.

"Things like this replenish my soul. They speak so much more eloquently of God's glory than I ever could. I feel humbled and exuberant and so much more." She leaned back against him and sighed at the sight of the white arch above the tumultuous falls. "It's like witnessing the earth praising its maker."

"Indeed."

They stood in tranquil communion for a while, enjoying the peace and beauty. Cameron cherished the nearness of Julia.

He did not know what she was thinking or feeling. He hardly knew his own mind or heart, except that for this one moment he had Julia in his arms and they seemed in perfect sync with each other, nature, and the Lord.

This, was his treasure. This moment. Whatever happened after, wherever their lives and God's will directed them, he would always have this moment buried deep within his heart.

He drew in the vanilla scent clinging to her hair and shut his eyes. The only thing that would make the moment more special was if he knew that Julia felt as he did.

"Cameron?"

"What is it, Julia?"

"The God who created all this could do wondrous things with me, if I let him. That's what you've been trying to tell me, isn't it?"

He turned her to him, placed his hand beneath her chin, and smiled. "You can do many things, Julia, but God can do so much more through you."

"If I surrender." She turned again to face the falls. The glimmering white mist arced in all its splendor in the full moon's light. "It's like this river."

"How's that?"

"A river, all the force of flowing water, wears down stone; cuts through the earth; nourishes plants, animals, and people, always moving on relentlessly, always working. Then it comes to this place where the earth and plants and stones fall away. For all its constant exertion, Cameron, the river doesn't make the moonbow."

She clasped her fingers around his and squeezed gently. "The moonbow happens when the river lets go."

There was nothing more to add to her analogy so he simply

195

stood there with her a while longer, thinking, absorbing the surroundings.

Finally, he shifted away.

"Is something wrong?" she asked.

Nothing that being able to hold you forever wouldn't fix. He shook his head. "Nothing is wrong, but we need to get back. I have an early day planned."

"You do?"

You do, she had said. Not *we* do as he had braced himself to hear. Perhaps Julia had really begun to let go of her need to be in on everything—if only just a bit. He ran his hand through his hair. "Yes, I do. I have to scout around a bit in the morning. I have a hunch about something."

"Oh?" She stepped back, close enough to fill the shelter of his arms, but he resisted the urge to embrace her.

Instead, he explained his thinking on the case in an almost inaudible whisper. "I keep going over in my mind some of the things my nephew said on the phone."

"Yes?"

"I made the connection when I found the note in the white car and finally realized they'd be heading here." He stole a quick peek around them to ensure that no one was eavesdropping.

"Just as your nephew had hinted in his phone calls? Reminding his mother to think of him on spring break—which they'd planned on spending right here," she supplied. "But you made that connection already and had this place staked out, Cameron."

"But I was thinking of them coming here to hide, not to find something already hidden."

"You think your friend suspected the gold was here before he ever stole that note?" Her hand pressed against the padding of his thick parka.

"Could be."

"Well, it makes sense since your father had been the one to tell everyone about it. So why didn't your friend just come down here?"

"Cat and mouse," he reminded her.

"Which are you?"

He arched an eyebrow. "Depends on your point of view. But if a certain 'cat' had been stalking me—and he had—he might be the kind of feline who feared taking the bait and finding a red herring."

She placed her hand on his chest and tipped her face up, her inviting lips curved. "Is this the way you spy types always talk?"

"Yes, we try to work in the buzz words whenever we can. That's how we spot one another," he teased, grateful for the levity. "Do you like it?"

"It's dreamy," she cooed through her sly smile. "Tell me more—and start with why you have to go scouting around."

"Trying to pry more vital information out of me, eh?"

"It's useless to resist my charms," she purred in an accent stolen straight from a bad cold-war spy spoof.

Despite the cornball routine they were playing, he had to admit her last remark had some truth to it. One look from those eyes and he was ready to tell her just about anything.

"If you must know," he said, "I've been bothered by the fact that all the boy's clues fit. He talked of southern fried chicken."

"Kentucky is south of Ohio and famous for its fried chicken," she said.

"Exactly. And he emphasized the word *following*."

"A warning that you were being followed?"

He nodded. "And then he told me exactly what to do to speed things along—get moving."

"You aren't kicking yourself because you didn't pick up on that right away, are you?"

"I was too focused on my own plan. I should have listened more carefully from the start." He forced down the wave of guilt rising in his stomach. "But that's behind me now. I have to move forward."

"By scouting around?"

"Yes."

"Where?"

He glanced at the base of the falls. "One thing didn't fit with the rest of Devin's hints—the continued reference to fishing."

"You're going fishing?"

"No." He shook his head. "But I think my friend is—for gold."

Julia sat up in her bed and stretched her arms over her head. For the first time in many years she could actually appreciate the words from the psalm: "This is the day which the Lord has made; let us rejoice and be glad in it."

She smiled. Who would have thought that letting go of her drive to do too much would bring such joy?

Cameron, that's who. She gazed up at the white ceiling and sighed. Cameron O'Dea. How blessed she was to have him in her life.

She laughed at the memory of his face last night when she had told him she didn't need to go with him on his scouting trip. He'd gaped at her in disbelief. He'd checked his hearing. He'd made a crack about her secretly scheming to arise before dawn, chart out the entire park, then present him with a strategic operational grid and relief map. Then he'd grinned *that* grin.

Her heart stirred at the recollection. She clutched the covers to her chest. How blessed—but for how long?

She chased away the temptation to worry over how soon she would be losing Cameron. She would not let worry ruin her day. Instead, she would give her concerns to the Lord.

She shut her eyes and offered a moment of silent praise, then sighed.

For the first morning in oh so long, she awakened from a truly restful night's sleep to no pressure, no responsibility, nothing but peace. She bit her lip and recalled the prayer for peace she had uttered on her doorstep—just before Shaughnessy had shown up.

She shuddered, then hugged her arms tightly around her body. She'd found peace in a new way of practicing her faith, and yet Shaughnessy was still out there. That thought unsettled her a bit.

"Miss Reed?" A brisk, businesslike knock jarred her from her thoughts.

She jumped, her legs jerking under the cool sheets.

"What is it, Carl?" she asked, her hand pressed to her T-shirt. Thanks to her new attitude, Julia had even made friends with her bodyguard.

"It's almost time for me to go off shift. Do you think it would be all right if I went now so I can still get in on the hot breakfast bar?"

"Sure, Carl. Go ahead."

"Cameron just came in, and he said he'd get cleaned up real fast and grab you some breakfast and bring it up."

"Thanks, Carl." She wondered if he could hear the contentment in her tone.

She threw back the covers and climbed out of bed, wanting to be dressed before Cameron showed up.

Jeans. Camp shirt. Socks. She wriggled into each item in haste, then turned to her personal grooming in leisure. The hard plastic bristles of her hairbrush made her scalp tingle as she stroked through her thick, black curls. Her lotion saturated her cheeks and chin and throat with cool softness. She inhaled the subtle scent, then let it out slowly.

She rarely wore makeup, but today she decided on a touch of mascara and a bit of lip gloss to complement her buoyed spirits.

She stood back from herself in the mirror and surveyed the results.

"You," she waggled one finger at her reflection, "look more like a woman in love than one steeped in international intrigue."

Love. She put her hand to her lips but, of course, the dreaded "L-word" was already out there. She watched as her pupils dilated and the flush of happy color drained from her face. Her upbeat surge of energy oozed out of her body, leaving her knees weak and her arms made of lead. Could her feelings for Cameron have already gone that far?

Had she been so foolish as to allow herself to fall for a man she could never have? Attraction, yes, she understood how that could have happened. Respect, of course. Even a passing affection might slip by her emotional defenses. But love?

"Love?" she whispered to the image of her stunned face. "It can't be."

"Julia?"

Her name, refined by the lilting Irish of the hushed male voice, stirred something deep within her.

Maybe she did love Cameron O'Dea, but that didn't mean she could—should—let him know it.

"Um, just a minute, Cameron." She lurched for the hiking boots he had given her, deciding it best to meet him ready to go rather than to allow him inside the close quarters.

She tucked one shoe under her arm then lifted her foot and set to work getting the other shoe.

He knocked lightly a few times. Paused, then knocked again.

She began to hop furiously around, trying to work her toes

inside the stiff new shoe. She tried and failed, tugged at her sagging sock, then tried again.

A barrage of light taps fell against the locked door.

Her heart seemed intent to mimic the insistent rat-a-tat-tat. Cameron wasn't usually so impatient. She hopped up and down, struggling with the shoe. "Just a minute. I've almost got—"

The shoe slipped from her grasp and thumped on the carpeted floor, bumping her shin along the way.

"Julia!" he rasped. Probably he wanted to hurry in before he drew a lot of attention.

"Oh, all right." She tossed the second shoe alongside its mate and hurried to the door, confident she now looked more battle-fatigued than love struck. "But I'm warning you, when you hustle a girl around like this, you'd better be ready to back yourself up with a really terrific surprise."

She flung open the door.

"Surprise." Michael Shaughnessy grinned.

"Do you want coffee with that, sir?"

Cameron squinted down at the ample breakfast he'd ordered on Julia's behalf. "I've never seen the lass drink coffee, but that doesn't mean she wouldn't like a cup on a fine spring morning like this."

"Perhaps if you took up a serving pot of hot water and a selection of instant coffees and teas?" The young man held up a small stainless steel pot with a black handle. "Or we have some really good flavored coffees."

"Flavored?"

"Irish mocha creme," the waiter said, lifting the small packet up as though tempting a pup with a treat.

Cameron smiled. "Well, now, how can I refuse that?"

As the young man prepared the sweet-smelling brew, he

edged closer to Cameron, as if creeping into his confidence. "You're looking for dead bodies, aren't you, sir?"

The question so took Cameron aback, all he could manage was to blink at the young man and mutter, "Bodies?"

"It's okay. You can trust me." The young man with the serious brown eyes and the name badge identifying him as James sidled closer. "I saw you go out with several park security officers before dawn this morning. I guessed from all the trail charts and terrain maps that you were looking for something."

The inference, despite the wrong conclusion, made Cameron freeze.

"And when some guests came back and said that security had blocked off parts of the park, it didn't take much to put it all together." James glanced to the left, to the right, then to the left one more time.

Cameron felt compelled to do the same.

When James spoke again, it was a subdued whisper from the corner of his mouth. "Gotta be bodies. Every few years you hear of some maniac burying bodies in some secluded park somewhere. I figured this year it was our turn."

"You watch a lot of television, don't you, son?"

"I get it. You can't talk about the case until you've got some evidence—a *body* of evidence, maybe?"

Cameron shook his head and picked up the silver plate cover on the counter. He placed it over Julia's breakfast.

This was the last thing he needed this morning, some zealous kid thinking he'd stumbled into an episode of a true crime drama. James and his misinformation could well cause problems for Cameron and his real case. The young man's suggestion that the police were digging up anything could spread through the lodge staff, then on to the guests, and then to other tourists and further.

Imagine Michael's reaction to that, he thought.

Imagine it, indeed.

The notion hit Cameron like a spark on spilled gasoline. Once ignited it spread though his mind so fast he could hardly contain it.

Where do you think you'd find a pot of gold? His father's dying words had echoed in Cameron's ears throughout the whole trip. *At the end of a rainbow.* The obvious answer, the answer that had led Cameron, on a whim, to the Lucky Lotto billboard, would direct Michael's path as well. If Michael thought the gold was in the park, then it had to lie at the end of the moonbow. And Michael had to intend to fish it out. But how?

The question haunted Cameron as he'd walked the trails and scoured the areas near the bottom of the falls. How could Michael hope to retrieve the gold with so many people always about? He didn't have the resources a man in Cameron's position had. He couldn't call on the police or park security to cordon off trails or allow him access to restricted areas.

But Michael never intended to do any of those things. He intended for Cameron to find the gold and retrieve it, then to swap it for Devin. Nice and neat.

Cat and mouse.

Cameron eyed the solemn-faced James. He didn't want to lie to the lad, and fortunately, thanks to an overactive imagination, he wouldn't have to—really. Just a few well-chosen words and Cameron could set a tidy little trap for his childhood friend.

"All right, James. You've got me." Cameron reached into his pocket and flashed his ID and badge.

"Interpol?" The kid's voice cracked like a dry reed in the wind. "For real?"

"For real." He returned his identification to his pocket.

"Then I was right."

"Part right, my boy. Only part." Cameron clamped his hand down on the protruding bones of the boy's skinny shoulder.

"We're not looking for bodies."

"What then?"

He leaned in. "Can I trust you?"

James tugged at the bottom of his black vest and squared his shoulders. "With your very life, sir."

Cameron cocked an eyebrow and struggled not to laugh. "Let's hope it doesn't come to that, son. Let's hope it doesn't come to that."

Cameron finally eased a chuckle out as he carried Julia's tray up the stairs to her room. Young James had fallen hook, line, and sinker for his fish tale. The boy's awe-struck expression had made clear that the young man had taken in every detail, especially the ones Cameron had wanted repeated—that the trails would be cleared in the early afternoon and no one, including park security, would be allowed in a certain area until further notice. That would give enough time for the rumor to spread and for Michael to find a suitable hiding place in the wooded area to lie in wait.

Now, Cameron could only trust to God that the plan would work out as he had foreseen it.

"Top o' the morning to you, good sir." Cameron gave a quick head bob of acknowledgment to Julia's day shift bodyguard. "I trust everything is fine here."

"Far as I know." The man didn't move from his spot two feet away and to the right of her door. "Been pretty quiet in there, but Carl said the lady was awake when he left."

Cameron stopped, the breakfast tray balanced across one forearm. "What do you mean, when Carl left? Weren't you here then?"

"Um, no, sir. He went down to breakfast a few minutes before I came on duty. We crossed paths in the dining room, and he briefed me on the situation there."

The stainless steel dish cover clattered as Cameron clutched at the tray. He gritted his teeth. "Carl left his post?"

"I'm sure everything's all right, sir."

"It had better be." Cameron shoved the tray at the unfamiliar guard, then lifted his fist to pound on Julia's door.

"Julia?" His hand came down with enough force to rattle the window sills, but his fist only glanced off the shuddering wood as the force propelled the door open.

"Julia?" He stepped inside, the bodyguard on his heels.

"Is she in the bathroom?" the other man asked.

In two booming steps, Cameron reached the open bathroom door. "She's not here."

"I'll alert park security," the man said. "If you're sure she didn't just go out for a walk or something harmless like that?"

Cameron's gaze fell on the new hiking boots tossed haphazardly on the floor. He glanced around in hopes the old loafers he'd replaced were missing. He saw the battered toes of the old shoes sticking out from inside the closet.

"I'm sure. Make the call."

The bodyguard excused himself, leaving Cameron alone in the vacant room, with nothing but gut-wrenching guilt and the subtle scent of vanilla.

~ 16 ~

The afternoon sun blazed down on Cameron's back. The cool, wispy clouds of the morning's damp fog had burned away and the air smelled of earth and water.

Before him, the Cumberland River plunged sixty feet down into a frothy turmoil. The sound of the falls rumbled in his ears at odds with the throbbing pulse in his temples. He lifted his head to survey the surroundings.

He seemed alone on the sun-dappled riverbank. He prayed that was not the case. He squinted across the water, using his hand to shade his eyes from the piercing glare. He could not see Michael, nor feel his friend's eyes upon him.

Yet he felt something. Anxiety, yes. And that gnawing guilt that had never quite left him since Devin had been taken, now amplified by Julia's kidnapping. He also admitted to himself the regret of having involved lovely Julia at all in his family's difficulties. If he had read his nephew's messages correctly from the start, Julia would be safe at work in St. Patrick's Shelter.

Of course, then he would never have had the chance to get to know her as he had. So that regret was tempered with gratitude.

Still, this feeling nagging deep inside him was something else. Something he couldn't quite name. He glanced toward the falls and caught in one breathtaking moment the sun catching the fine mist. What by night formed a moonbow, by day blessed the area with a faint, shimmering rainbow. A slow smile eased over Cameron's lips.

He thought of Julia's analogy. The moonbow, or today the rainbow, only happened when the river "let go."

For all Cameron's attempts to persuade Julia in the ways of surrendering to the Lord, now he understood. He had needed the lesson as much as she did.

For most of his life he had held on to a shame that was not his to bear. He had struggled to be worthy when no human act could ever make him so. He had sought a treasure that he did not want, one that would never make him happy.

And today, he would let go.

"Where do you find a pot of gold?" he whispered to the nearly transparent arc of colors.

He moved to the water's edge.

The breeze stirred his hair and swept a fine mist of water over him. He crouched on a pile of river rocks, wedging his feet into the crevices to keep from sliding. Tiny droplets clung to his hands, his jeans, and shimmied on the hairs of his forearms exposed by the pushed-back sleeves of his sweatshirt.

He gripped a flat stone jutting out from the river's edge. He clenched his teeth. Then he plunged his arm into the icy, churning waters.

Please, Lord, make this work. For Devin and now Julia and even for Michael, let this end here, today.

He drew in a deep breath, thinking he might have to stick his head under to locate the fake pot of gold planted during the minutes after he'd discovered Julia missing. Then his fingers skimmed the slick ceramic rim of the make-do container. He stretched. He strained. His fingertips squeaked off the smooth surface, then he finally latched on.

This was it. If he was right that Michael was watching him, he'd know any minute now.

"I wish I could tell you how sorry I am, Devin, that I just handed you over to Shaughnessy like that." Julia strained against the coarse, prickly rope binding her hands to the side mirror of the green four-wheel drive they'd known Shaughnessy had rented. The edge of the passenger window cut into her underarm as she leaned farther out of the vehicle to slacken the restraints. The rope loosened enough to let her blood circulate again. She winced as the red scrapes circling her wrists came alive with burning pain.

"Don't fret yourself none over it, ma'am. 'Twas only into the hands of me own uncle you handed me." Unlike Julia, the spry redheaded boy did not fight his constraints. He sprawled out over the soft upholstery of the back seat like a typical youngster vegging out in front of a TV.

"Well, he's not really your uncle," she said, rubbing her ankles together in hopes of relaxing the knots of rope there as well. "And you did try to get away. If I hadn't been in such a hurry and had listened to you more closely—"

The boy sighed. "'Tis true. You could have handled it better, lass. In fact, we both of us wouldn't be in this stew if you had listened to me."

She stopped her struggling. Obviously all the males in the O'Dea family carried the arrogant-obnoxious gene. She rolled her eyes. "On the other hand, let's take a moment to recall what you were saying, young man. That leprechaun nonsense?"

"Oh. That."

She glanced at the boy in the rearview mirror and watched

as his fair skin turned as red as a boiled lobster.

"Yes, that," she said.

He squirmed. "Well, I, um. You see, my thoughts were on the gold and when your husband brought the matter up—"

"My husband?" She saw her brows dart down and a deep crease form between them. "Oh, you mean Craig? He isn't my husband, he's the assistant director where I work."

"Ah, that explains it then."

"Explains what?"

"Oh, nothing. Just something me mother said, that's all."

"What? What did your mother say? Something about me?"

"Not about you exactly."

"Oh."

"About you and me Uncle Cam."

Her breath stilled low in her throat. She blinked and tossed back her hair and forced the air out slowly. "I'm not sure I want to hear it then."

"Trust me. You don't. That is, unless—" He cocked his head, his green eyes sparkling.

The gesture reminded her of Cameron. Apparently, they also shared an Irish imp-style sense of humor.

The boy stuck out his lower lip and frowned. "Naw, you wouldn't be interested."

"Try me."

"Me mother said that if all went well, 'twas more than family honor Uncle Cam would find in this folly. Said he might just find a family as well."

A chill crept over Julia's skin, raising it into a million goose-bumps. She shifted her shoulders against the upholstery, drew in the smell of old forest and new car and cleared her throat. "That could have been about getting you back or the three of you being together again or—" She looked at him sharply. "What makes you think it involved me?"

The boy shrugged. "No reason."

"Just a lucky leprechaun guess, I suppose."

"Could be." His smirk denied his ready reply. "Either way—doesn't mean no nevermind to me, you understand."

She tipped her nose up to get a better peek at the boy in the rearview mirror again. "Is that so?"

"Because lovely lady friend or no, my Uncle Cam, me mother, and meself are headin' back to Ireland when the trouble with the gold is settled."

That tidbit of information hit Julia like a smarting slap across the cheek. Why it would shock her so, she didn't care to speculate. She had known that Cameron would be gone as soon as he settled the matter of his nephew and the gold. She just hadn't realized, she supposed, that he would go so very far away. She dropped her gaze from the image in the mirror and murmured, "To stay?"

"Me mother hasn't decided yet for us. But my Uncle Cam—you know he never does stay one place too long. He's awfully old to be changing that now."

Julia thought of Cameron's fit, muscular body, of the vital energy he exuded, of his unlined face and intense green eyes. "Oh, yeah, I see your point, son. Your uncle is a regular old geezer."

Devin grunted in the universal language of young people that said he didn't appreciate her humor.

"Anyway—my point, when I started this whole crazy conversation, was to apologize for getting you kidnapped." She shut her eyes and laid her head back against the seat.

The boy grunted again, more a dismissive huff than an actual sound of disgust or annoyance.

"Even if the man is like a member of your family, this can't have been a pleasant experience for you," she went on. "And it hasn't been easy on your mother or your real uncle."

She heard the boy shifting in the seat behind her and opened her eyes to find him working his way into a sitting position.

"This part hasn't been such a trial, lass," he admitted, a grudging cross between a sneer and a smile on his face. Then his eyes lifted to meet her gaze in the mirror, and for the first time, his expression mellowed. "And I have to tell you, it has staved off the thing I've long dreaded. A thing that could be much, much worse."

Her stomach clenched. "When Cameron and Shaughnessy face off over the gold?"

Devin nodded.

"But they're old friends," she reminded the boy, with an encouraging smile that felt as forced as her words. "Really, now, how bad could it be?"

"If Uncle Cam surrenders the gold?" The boy gazed out the window a moment, seeming to try to assess the situation fairly. He sighed and shrugged again. "Not too bad, I guess. But if he doesn't surrender it—"

"What?" She sputtered out a laugh, her attempt at lightness betrayed by a panicky, shrill note. "What's the worst that could happen?"

The boy pressed his lips together. His green eyes darted to one side and then the other. Clearly, he had to consider the gravity of discussing this family matter with a stranger. Despite his confinement, Devin obviously had a deep affection for Shaughnessy, as he did for his uncle Cameron.

Julia understood how difficult it must be on someone so young to have his loyalties divided like this, then to have to choose between them. That's why it meant all the more when the boy raised his grim eyes to the mirror and held her gaze there for a few, pulsing heartbeats.

"Uncle Mike has a gun," he finally murmured.

She swallowed the gasp that rose to her lips. Her mind fumbled through a dozen thoughts without picking up on any one. She blinked and mumbled, "You don't think Shaughnessy would kill us, do you?"

"No." The boy shook his head, his expression earnest. "No, I don't think he'd ever do that."

"That's good." She sighed.

"Uncle Mike would never kill *us*."

The implication sent a blade of freezing fear through her gut.

She knew Cameron was a trained professional, but she also knew he had gone to great lengths to avoid any risk to his old friend. As she sat there, her heart slamming out a punishing pulse in her ears, she had to wonder. If it came to a showdown, would Cameron's loyalty to his friend and his willingness to surrender his fate to God ultimately cost him his life?

Cameron clasped the decoy pot to his stomach. He scrambled up the riverbank, aware that to convince Michael, he had to put on a credible show.

The tracks of his boot soles gripped the flat gray rocks as he made his way up along the side of the waterfall. If he intended to make a spectacle of himself, he thought, he should do it in the most visible spot possible.

At the top, on the edge of the falls, he paused. His fingers tightened against the wet ceramic surface. He straightened his back. He gazed down at the weighted pot and tried to conjure up a reaction for Michael's sake.

His mind went blank. A little more than a week ago, he'd have known exactly how to respond to the moment he first held the long-sought-after gold in his hands. Today, it all seemed so meaningless.

Julia's face flashed in his mind. His chest constricted. How could his priorities have changed so quickly?

He glanced below his rocky perch, to the falls hurtling down into frothing whiteness and he had his answer. Like the river, like Julia, once he had relinquished the struggle to win the gold, the Lord had given him something worth so much more.

The heaviness of both the bogus pot and the very hoax he hoped to perpetrate with it made his arms and his heart numb. If only he could find another way to reach Michael. If only he'd had his priorities straight before and could have approached his friend with this new outlook. If only—

"A penny for your thoughts, old friend—or should I suggest another type of coin. A gold coin, perhaps?"

The pure malevolence of the tone oozed over Cameron's taut nerves like slick, black oil over still, dark waters.

He twisted his neck to peer over his shoulder. "Michael. If I said I was surprised to see you here, I'd be lying."

"I told you—'twould be my shadow that fell across your back when you finally claimed the treasure." The afternoon sun glinted off the black barrel of his handgun.

Cameron tensed his abdomen against the handle of his own gun, thrust into his waistband beneath his sweatshirt. "So that's what it's come to, has it? That you'd threaten me with a gun? For what? A few gold coins you can never spend?"

"For sure an' I came armed, old friend. Just as I have no doubt that you did as well." He motioned with his gun. "Now, keep one hand on me gold and with the other hand throw down your weapon."

Cameron gritted his teeth. He tossed his gun with a soft thud onto a carpet of pine needles in a spot of dirt among the rocks. He supposed he should feel bested, but he felt relief instead. With the gun out of his reach, the temptation to use it was not as strong.

"Good. Good." Michael edged closer, kicking Cameron's gun farther away. "Now, if you'll just give me the gold."

He held out his hand.

Cameron's gaze dipped to the ruddy palm stretched out toward him. "First you tell me where Devin and Julia are."

"I don't think so." He waved the gun again. "I'm going to need every advantage possible to get out of this park—and then the country. And hostages make fine shields."

A shudder gripped Cameron from the core of his being. "You'd do that? With a boy who has been like a nephew to you?"

Michael slitted his eyes. His expression became a treacherous wince. "No harm has come to him and none will."

Cameron answered the hard gaze with one of his own. "And what about Julia?"

"I have no intention of harming the pretty lady—but whether or not I do, that remains in your hands." He pointed the handgun at the pot in Cameron's arms.

The thought of Julia in direct danger gave rise to a sour burning in Cameron's mouth. His mind blurred between his hope of redeeming his old friend and the need to rescue her. If he could reach Michael, he reasoned, maybe he could accomplish both.

"Michael, tell me this lunacy hasn't gone so far that you would think of hurting an innocent woman."

Shaughnessy angled his square chin upward. "I would do no such thing."

That was the Michael he once knew. Cameron relaxed a bit.

"Unless you force me to it," Michael added, his voice dripping venom. "If the woman comes to harm, you will bear the guilt, Cameron, not me."

Suddenly it became clear to Cameron why Michael had taken the chance of speaking to the bubble-haired Imogene—

even going so far as to get her phone number. He'd needed a second hostage all along because they both knew that the threat of Michael hurting Devin was practically nonexistent.

By bringing Julia along, by involving her at all, Cameron had provided Michael with the perfect human collateral against capture. A dull, throbbing anguish twisted in Cameron's chest at the thought of his own imprudent actions and the truly cowardly actions of his friend.

Only a truly vicious mind would have plotted such a thing. He narrowed his eyes at his once-closest friend.

"What's happened to you, man?" Cameron whispered, his head shaking. "Has the thirst for gold and glory choked out all that once was good in you?"

"I've told you, it isn't me, but you who holds the lady's fate in your hands."

"You and I both know the lady's fate is in greater hands than mine," Cameron said, the very thought giving him some comfort.

Michael grunted.

Cameron sighed and anchored the ceramic pot against his chest with his curved arm. "I can't believe there stands before me the same lad who took his first communion at my side, now with a gun aimed at me."

"Shut up and give me the gold." He stabbed the gun at Cameron, implying his patience had worn thin.

Cameron pressed on. "Have you gone so far around the bend, Michael, that not even the love of God can bring you back?"

Jagged copper highlights glinted in Michael's hair as he inched closer still, his eyes hard as flint and his face a grim mask. "I didn't come for a lecture, Cameron, I came for me treasure. It's mine. It's due me."

"It's not yours. And it's not the family's. It really has nothing to do with us, you know." Cumberland Falls resounded in his ears. He could feel its power under his feet.

"'Tis the prize of our forefathers."

"'Tis their curse. This gold and the want of it took everything they had from them—their dignity, their freedom, and eventually their lives."

"Don't you see, Cameron? That's why we deserve to lay claim to it." Michael took another cautious step closer to the water's edge. "'Tis the redemption of our family's honor."

Cameron chuckled.

Michael stopped his creeping progress. "What's so funny?"

"The truth."

"The—?"

"All these years, I've thought our lives were taking us in such very different paths. But we were more alike than not, Michael." Cameron scooted backward, relying on the traction of his boots to keep him from slipping on the damp rocks.

Michael watched with wary eyes but did not move.

"You thought you deserved to be the one to claim the gold," Cameron said. "I thought that I alone could retrieve it and redeem the family name. But what a pretty price we've both paid, haven't we, Michael?"

"I don't know what you mean."

Cameron could feel the spray of the crashing falls now. It left a dewy film over his hands, his face, his clothes. "I mean we followed what we thought were different paths and ended up at the same place, brought here by the same thing. Two lonely men with neither wife nor home nor children. Just this."

He wrapped his hands around the lip of the pot and held it up.

"Once I have that—" Michael pointed to the pot with the tip of the gun, "—the others will fall into place."

Cameron laughed a sharp laugh. "Now there's another

example of how alike we are, friend. I've told myself the same thing. Once the matter of the gold was settled, my life could begin. In the meantime, my life has been passing me by as I struggled away after this."

He gave the pot a shake. The spare change and rocks they'd planted in the container clanked and rattled.

Michael lapped at his lips like a famished man eyeing a feast, his voice gruff when he ordered, "Enough."

"Oh, I couldn't agree more. Enough." He glanced at the water that rushed toward the falls, then lost control in a beautiful, terrifying flood.

He shifted the pot into both hands, then slowly pushed it outward toward the gunman.

Michael extended his empty hand.

The sound of the falls swelled. The earth beneath their feet trembled. Rivulets ran down Cameron's cheeks and neck and as he turned his head away from Michael, the sun shot through the fine mist and the rainbow appeared.

"It's time to give up the struggle, Michael. Because I've recently learned an amazing thing." Cameron smiled and faced his longtime friend and nemesis. "The Lord makes wondrous things happen when we finally learn to let go."

He used the weight of the pot to swing it up and out. The ceramic slid easily from his grip.

"No!" Michael lunged, flinging the gun aside as he stretched out both his hands.

Cameron stepped in before Michael's desperate attempt to capture the pot sent him headfirst over the falls. In one fluid movement, Cameron caught the other man around the shoulders, pinning down his arms.

"It's over, Michael," he whispered. "After all this time, it's finally over."

✍ 17 ✍

W hen Irish eyes are smilin'—"

"Norman!" Julia pushed back from her desk and tossed the pencil from her cramping fingers.

"Yes, Julia?" Norman Wilson stuck his head in the door of her office and grinned like a cat who had just eaten a canary. Coarse hair, the color of burnished silver, poked out like close-cropped feathers from underneath his red baseball cap.

Despite her agitation at his choice of performance material, Julia had to smile at the man who had become her best volunteer as well as a good friend.

"Could you...you know?" She placed her index finger to her lips to ask for quiet.

He spread his arms wide. "Ah, Julia, can I help it if there's song in my heart?"

She supposed not. But why did it have to be that song?

"It's a lovely spring day," he said with a heartwarming exuberance. "The shelter is in great shape, we break ground today on phase two of our Help the Homeless Project, the Reds are at Riverside, and all is right with the world."

She could argue that last point. All was not right with *her* world.

Yes, these past few weeks had been busy and fruitful. Thanks to the groundwork laid by Cameron, and with Norman's dogged persistence in follow-up, they had recently branched out into a new project. Building would begin soon on a residential facility, designed to provide emergency aid for families, to keep them off the streets and get them back on their feet. That made her proud and she supposed it would also have made Cameron proud—to learn that she hadn't rushed in and assumed the responsibility for the new undertaking. In fact, she hadn't even asked to be a part of the selection committee for the facility's director.

But Cameron did not know that. He couldn't. After he had turned Shaughnessy over to the the FBI and freed Devin and her, they had taken a slow, awkward trip back to Cincinnati. Always aware of Devin's watchful eyes and ears, they hadn't spoken of anything personal.

By now, Julia had begun to wonder if there had ever been anything personal between them at all. Perhaps the loneliness of losing herself in the work of the shelter had made her see things that simply weren't there. And feel things that Cameron did not share.

She swallowed to force down the lump in her throat. It lodged hard and high in her chest, settling in with the dull ache she'd felt ever since she'd last heard a certain teasing Irish brogue.

She thought of his sweet but brief good-bye when she went to see his plane off. With Fiona and Devin beside him, he'd set off to do the thing he'd sought to accomplish for so long. The stolen coins would be returned—and so would his family's honor.

That had been over a month ago.

She forced out a shuddering sigh.

"Julia?" Norman came fully into the room. "You okay?"

"Sure." She lifted her chin and shook back the hair clinging to her cheeks. "Why shouldn't I be okay? I'm just a little—tired and testy."

"Sorry if my singing bothered you, then. I just sorta had this sudden outpouring of goodwill and optimism," he explained, touching the brim of his baseball cap.

"I don't mind you making a joyful noise while you do your work, Norman." She leaned back in her creaking swivel chair. "But could you, um, maybe pick a different song?"

"You miss him, don't you?"

"Who?" She batted her lashes and hoped she looked sufficiently perplexed.

"Okay, I get it." He held his hands up. "None of my business. I just hope your mood picks up a bit before the groundbreaking ceremony today."

The thought of going before the press and putting on a happy face rattled Julia. She wasn't much of an actor—that was Cameron's department. And this was Cameron's project, to keep the little ones from saying their good night prayers in a cafeteria, he had said when he'd suggested it.

The memory brought a tingle to the tip of her nose and a burning to her eyes. She set her jaw and swallowed hard. She would not cry. She refused to let these feelings dominate her. She blinked to battle back the tears.

The trick, she had learned, was simply not to let herself dwell on thoughts of Cameron.

How could she go to this event and not think of him? How could she think of him and not feel blue? She whisked her hand through her hair and groaned out a burdened sigh. "Actually, I'm pretty busy here today. I don't know if I can make the time—"

"Oh, no, you don't."

"Oh, no, she doesn't what?" Craig sauntered into the office.

"She's trying to back out of going to the groundbreaking ceremony for phase two," Norman accused, his face crinkled in a disapproving expression.

"Julia!" Craig marched up to her desk and plunked his fist on top of her paperwork. "You have to go today, and that's that."

"Why?" she demanded.

"Because St. Patrick's is the parent facility of this project," he said, gesturing boldly. "You can't just not show up at the phase two groundbreaking."

"Then you go in my stead."

He shook his head. "This is upper echelon all the way—directors, CEOs, civic group presidents, the mayor. No one else is sending an assistant and you can't either. With a group like that nobody will be impressed by a second banana."

"Second banana." Norman hooted laugh. "Now there's a doozy of a nickname for you, kid."

Craig raised one finger at Norman and issued a warning with good humor. "Well, If I'm second banana, what does that make you, pal?"

"Anything else would sound more *appealing*," Norman countered.

Julia winced. "Another bad pun like that one and I'm going to have to ask you both to split."

"Oh, my word, Craig, do you see that?" Norman feigned shock.

"What?" Craig followed the other man's line of vision, zeroing his gaze in on Julia's face.

"A smile!" Norman tipped back his cap and squinted. "If I'm not mistaken—and I could be since it's been so long since any of us has had an actual Julia Reed smile-sighting—that's a bonafide grin."

"You know, you may be right."

"Okay, you two got me. I admit it, you jollied me up a bit." She held her hands up in surrender. "Happy now?"

"We won't be truly happy until you promise to come to the groundbreaking ceremony today," Norman said.

"They're going to introduce the new project director," Craig sing-songed, as if that might prove too tempting to pass up.

"They've hired someone already?" She sat up.

That news did shed a new light on the situation. She really should make an appearance if just to thank the right people and meet the person she'd be spending a great deal of time with.

"It's a golden opportunity," Norman chimed in.

Julia stiffened at his choice of words. *Golden.* It made her think of the gleam in Cameron's hair when the sun hit it just right and of the mischievous glint in his dazzling emerald eyes. She slumped in her seat.

"I've got so much pressing business here today—"

"Wee-oo. Wee-oo." Craig placed one hand to his lips like a mouthpiece of a trumpet. "Waffle alert. Lady in sector five is thinking of backing out on her commitments."

She straightened her spine. "I do not back out on my commitments."

"Then I guess we'll see you at the new project site in an hour." Craig gave her a quick salute and slipped out the door.

Norman tipped his cap and did the same.

"I am not up to this," Julia growled through gritted teeth as she tottered on unaccustomed high heels through an open field. She tugged at the collar and then the sleeve of the new kelly green linen suit she had bought just for this presentation.

"You can do this, Julia," Craig assured her as they walked

toward a cluster of cameras and dignitaries.

"You'll be as terrific as you look." Norman beamed from his place at her elbow.

"Well, I'm wearing this fancy outfit under protest, you understand. If you two hadn't shamed me into buying it, I'd be in my favorite jeans and a comfy T-shirt." Her legs wobbled as she stepped along the uneven ground. "I feel silly. I think I should be dressed like I came here to work."

"You should be dressed, Miss Shelter Director, like you came here to do business." Craig waved his hand. "It's an entirely different thing."

"Absolutely." Norman's short legs did double time to match their long strides. "Besides, don't you want to look your best when you see—"

Craig cut him off with an abrupt slashing motion across the base of his own throat.

"What's going on here?" She paused, and her heels began to sink into the lush grassy ground. "When I see what?"

"Um, when you see this." Craig extended his arm in a sweeping motion that encompassed the whole chaotic scene. "We really did it up right, Julia. Press, CEOs, city officials. The Wacky Wake Up Weather Guy."

She narrowed her eyes to tell Craig she hadn't bought his story, then glanced at the assembled crowd. Everyone he'd mentioned was there—and then some. A semicircle of people she'd never seen before stood in expensive suits and dresses around a white-flagged stake in the dry ground. Each of them held authentic gardening spades, spray-painted a gaudy gold.

As she approached, an anxious young man rushed up to her with an identical spade in his hands. He thrust it toward Julia. "So glad you got here, Miss Reed."

He escorted her to the end of the semicircle, pausing to whisper in her ear. "Now, the mayor is going to give a short

speech, and the CEO of the funding company is going to introduce the new director. After that, they'll join the group here,
and all of you will push your spades into the ground. That will
make a great shot for the newspaper."

She nodded to let him know she understood, but he had
already scurried up to the makeshift podium to signal the
beginning of the media event.

The mayor's speech was a benign blend of humor and
pathos, ending with a plea for a better world and a reminder
that the way to build that world was by voting. He didn't say
"voting for me" could improve the world, but even Julia, in her
fog of boredom and despondency, got that message.

She smiled politely as he passed in front of her to take his
place on the other side of the half-circle of groundbreakers.

The CEO of the company who had provided the start-up
funds for the project stepped up to the microphone.

Yadda, yadda. Blah, blah, blah. He probably said something
more significant than that, but to Julia's ears, it didn't sound
much different.

Her feet hurt. The sun scorched the top of her head. The
wind whipped her hair into her eyes, and to top it all off, she
missed Cameron.

And still the CEO droned on, extolling the virtues of his
company's philanthropy.

Life goes on, she told herself. Like the river, like the Lord's
work, every day it just keeps flowing ever onward. And for all
her brave talk of letting go and surrendering herself to God's
will, sometimes it was all she could do not to let the old ways
barge in and use every resource available to find Cameron. Find
him, she thought, and then demand that he tell her why he
never called or wrote—or seemed to care at all what had happened to her.

"And that is why it is with great pride—"

Julia perked up. That sounded like the beginning of the end of one insufferably long speech.

"That we have chosen a director to oversee this project—"

Finally, Julia said to herself as she stretched her neck up just a bit to get a better view through the crowd, *something interesting*.

"Who embodies the goals of our generous corporation towards ending the blight of homelessness in our city—"

Just say it already, she mused.

"Former Interpol agent and hero in his home country and locally—"

Julia's heart stopped. *Don't say what I think you're going to say*. Not even her pulse registered in her ears as the new director's name echoed through her mind and body.

"Cameron O'Dea."

Sunlight glinted off the golden curls on Cameron's head as he moved from the blur of the crowd to shake the CEO's hand. He exchanged some pleasantries with the businessman beyond the reach of the microphone, then stepped up to acknowledge the enthusiastic applause with a wave.

Stunned, Julia could neither think nor react. She just stood there with her mouth gaping wide, as the man with the brilliant green eyes fixed his gaze on her and came to take his place at her side.

He smiled down at her.

She blinked. Her muscles were as limp as rags and yet her posture was rigid. She wanted to ask him how or why or what was going on, but the connection between her brain and her lips failed. She just stared.

"And now, let us break ground on this new and worthwhile project!" the CEO announced.

Every other golden spade crunched into the barren ground. The air filled with the sent of fresh earth. A cheer went up.

226

Julia just stared.

"Sweet Julia?" Cameron whispered.

"What?" she murmured, her gaze caressing his cheeks, his lips, his eyes.

"You need to really dig in with that spade." He motioned to the tool leaning lifeless against her as her hands curled around the handle. "You know, faith can move mountains, but sometimes it has to do it one shovelful of dirt at a time. And somebody has to hold the shovel."

She smiled. "It's really you, isn't it? You're really here."

"I'm really here. And I'm really here to stay. I've resigned my position with Interpol, and I want to make Cincinnati my home." He reached over and helped her push down on the ceremonial spade.

The blade cut into the soft soil, crumbling the ground into dirt and clods.

Julia kept her eyes on him. She inhaled the scent of him. savored the heat of his body and the way he made her feel protected and safe.

"Cameron?"

"Hmm?" He met her gaze.

Those eyes spoke to her just as they had the very first day. She saw in them goodness and humor and just enough human frailty to make him a godly man.

"I'm glad you're back," she said.

"I'm glad to be back."

"No, I mean I'm really glad that you're back."

"And I'm really glad to be back, sweet Julia. Whatever the future brings, we can leave that in God's hands."

"I agree," she whispered. "We'll do what we can with what we're given and as for the rest—we'll just have to let go."

"There are some things, sweet Julia, that a man can't let go of."

"Like what?"

"His principles, his heart's desire, and a woman who shares them both. And it doesn't hurt if that woman is strong, and smart, and beautiful, and—"

He took her in his arms and kissed her.

The crowd cheered.

The kiss came to a quick conclusion.

Julia ducked her head to hide the warm blush washing over her face.

Cameron nodded to thank the crowd for their support.

"I hate to be a spoilsport, but can I ask you all to lift another spade of dirt?" A photographer gestured to the group. "We didn't get the picture the first time."

The shovel brigade gladly obliged, and as the spades hit the dirt, someone called out.

"Hey, Mr. O'Dea, what do we do if one of us hits buried gold like Miss Reed did?"

"If anyone digs up a pot of gold on this lot—"

The hushed attention of the crowd fixed on the man with the velvet voice and the sparkling Irish eyes.

"He can keep it." He gave one hand a dismissive flick, while the other held Julia close. "I've got the only treasure I'll ever need right here."

Epilogue

W hy, I do believe that this is the second St. Patrick's Day in a row that you haven't worn green, sweet Julia."

"That just goes to show how much you know, Cameron O'Dea."

Julia placed her slippered foot on the edge of a chair. With the most delicate of care, she gathered the hem of her dress in her fingers. The lace and taffeta skirt rustled as she drew it up slowly to reveal the blue satin and lace garter above her knee. A vivid green four-leaf clover encased in a gold-trimmed bubble dangled against her white-stockinged leg.

"Why, Mrs. O'Dea," Cameron murmured as appreciation glimmered in his green eyes.

She smiled back at him, a quiet, sly smile.

He reached for the garter, in accordance with the American custom, and eased it slowly down her long leg.

The gathered guests, so many that they had decided to hold the reception in the cafeteria at St. Patrick's Shelter, murmured, laughed, and applauded at the couple's display.

Julia lowered her lashes. She felt a warm blush tingle on her

cheeks. Her foot came to rest on the tile floor, her dress swaying gently as it fell back into place.

Beside her, Cameron swirled the garter around on his finger
and then flung it to the waiting bachelors.

A shuffle ensued. Craig Davis emerged with the trophy. The
crowd cheered but none more loudly than his longtime, long-
suffering girlfriend.

The party fell back into its merry revelry.

"Now that I've removed that wee bit of green, you're once
again flaunting the tradition of my favorite holiday," Cameron
warned.

"How do you know?" She cocked an eyebrow at him. "I
could still be wearing green—in a place hidden by all this fluff
and finery."

He pulled her close to him and bent his head to whisper
against her temple. "Are you now, lass?"

Joy radiated through her entire body as she cherished the
feel of her husband's arms around her. She giggled.

Julia Reed O'Dea, the grim girl who thought she alone could
save people from themselves, giggled. Julia marvelled at the
changes she had undergone in the past year.

She placed a hand on Cameron's shoulder and murmured
into his ear. "I guess you won't know for sure how much green
I'm wearing—or not wearing—until tonight."

"How long did you say we have to stay at this reception?"

She laughed again and gave him a quick kiss. "And to think,
a year ago we hadn't even shared a kiss, and now—"

"Yes we did," he argued. "We had our first kiss a year ago
this very day, my dear."

"No." She shook her head, her sheer veil flowing over the
black coils of her hair. "We almost kissed, but we were rudely
interrupted by a couple of phone calls."

"That's right." He frowned at the memory. "Which reminds

me, you didn't give Craig the phone number of our hotel, did you?"

"Nope." She wrapped her arms around him and leaned her head back. "I trust him. He's very capable and I know he can handle things on his own."

Cameron smiled, no doubt, at the change he'd helped bring about in her.

"And what about you, sir?" She poked a finger into his chest. "Are you going to bring your cellular phone?"

He narrowed his eyes and smirked. "What cellular phone?"

"Good."

"Besides, if my workers need to get in touch with me—"

"No."

"What?"

"For the next week, dear husband, the only one getting in touch with you is me."

His green eyes flashed.

"As I was saying—" He plucked up her hand and grazed a kiss over her knuckles. "My workers don't need to get in touch with me."

She laughed and stroked the soft waves of hair on his bent head.

Across the room Fiona and Devin waved at her. She smiled at her new family.

"Happy, my dear?" Cameron asked his new bride.

"More than I could ever have imagined myself being."

"It's amazing what the Lord can do when you leave things in his hands, isn't it?"

"Yes," she agreed. "And whatever twists and turns lie in our future, if we have faith enough to surrender to his will, God can do beautiful and inspiring things with our lives."

"And with our lives together," Cameron reminded her.

She rested her hand against his cheek and sighed, content to know that she would spend the rest of her days gazing into those heart-stopping Irish eyes.

∿ ∿ ∿ ∿ ∿

Michael Shaughnessy isn't out of the lives of the O'Dea family! Watch for his story in *Irish Rogue*, coming this fall.

Dear Reader,

When I was asked to write an open letter, I admit I felt a bit like the hero in my story when a microphone was shoved in front of him and he was asked to "say something Irish." I hope I do a better job representing myself than he did!

I first imagined Julia Reed, a woman of courage with a fierce desire to help others, and Cameron O'Dea, with those brilliant green eyes and easy laughter, years ago. I set their story aside when I realized they lacked a depth needed to share their love story. Still, I always hoped I would have the chance to give them their Christian spirits, their adventure, and their happy ending. I am so grateful to Palisades for allowing them—and me, of course—this opportunity.

I have been asked what lesson a romance novel teaches us. What "good" does it do? My ready answer is that it shows first and foremost that love is not a disposable commodity, that people matter, and if two people work together, they can form a bond that will last a lifetime. To be able to add the fuller dimension of faith to the characters is an exciting bonus that gives the unfurling relationship, the storyline, and me a fresh new outlook.

I enjoyed bringing Julia and Cameron to life, listening in on their squabbling, laughing with them, and learning from them. I hope you did as well.

Blessings!

Annie Jones

Write to Annie Jones at Palisades c/o Questar Publishers, Inc.
P.O. Box 1720, Sisters, Oregon 97759

Look for Barbara Jean Hicks' next novel,
China Doll, in June 1998.

～ ～ ～ ～ ～

Georgine has long resigned herself to growing old alone.
Does she still have a chance at romance—and motherhood?

Palisades...Pure Romance

～ Palisades ～

Reunion, Karen Ball
Refuge, Lisa Tawn Bergren
Torchlight, Lisa Tawn Bergren
Treasure, Lisa Tawn Bergren
Chosen, Lisa Tawn Bergren
Firestorm, Lisa Tawn Bergren
Wise Man's House, Melody Carlson
Arabian Winds, Linda Chaikin (Premier)
Cherish, Constance Colson
Chase the Dream, Constance Colson (Premier)
Angel Valley, Peggy Darty
Sundance, Peggy Darty
Love Song, Sharon Gillenwater
Antiques, Sharon Gillenwater
Song of the Highlands, Sharon Gillenwater (Premier)
Secrets, Robin Jones Gunn
Whispers, Robin Jones Gunn
Echoes, Robin Jones Gunn
Sunsets, Robin Jones Gunn
Coming Home, Barbara Jean Hicks
Snow Swan, Barbara Jean Hicks
Irish Eyes, Annie Jones
Glory, Marilyn Kok
Sierra, Shari MacDonald
Forget-Me-Not, Shari MacDonald
Diamonds, Shari MacDonald
Westward, Amanda MacLean
Stonehaven, Amanda MacLean
Everlasting, Amanda MacLean

Promise Me the Dawn, Amanda MacLean (Premier)
Kingdom Come, Amanda MacLean
Betrayed, Lorena McCourtney
Escape, Lorena McCourtney
Voyage, Elaine Schulte

A Christmas Joy, Darty, Gillenwater, MacLean
Mistletoe, Ball, Hicks, McCourtney
A Mother's Love, Bergren, Colson, MacLean

THE PALISADES LINE

Ask for them at your local bookstore. If the title you seek is not in stock, the store may order you a copy using the ISBN listed.

Wise Man's House, Melody Carlson
ISBN 1-57673-070-0
Kestra McKenzie, a young widow trying to make a new life for herself, thinks she has found the solidity she longs for when she purchases her childhood dream house—a stone mansion on the Oregon Coast. Just as renovations begin, a mysterious stranger moves into her caretaker's cottage—and into her heart.

Sunsets, Robin Jones Gunn
ISBN 1-57673-103-0
Alissa Benson loves her job as a travel agent. But when the agency has computer problems, they call in expert Brad Phillips. Alissa can't wait for Brad to fix the computers and leave—he's too blunt for her comfort. So she's more than a little upset when she moves into a duplex and finds out he's her neighbor!

Snow Swan, Barbara Jean Hicks
ISBN 1-57673-107-3
Life hasn't been easy for Toni Ferrier. As an unwed mother and a recovering alcoholic, she doesn't feel worthy of anyone's love. Then she meets Clark McConaughey, who helps her launch her business aboard the sternwheeler Snow Swan. Sparks fly between them, but if Clark finds out the truth about Toni's past, will he still love her?

Irish Eyes, Annie Jones
ISBN 1-57673-108-1
When Julia Reed finds a young boy, who claims to be a leprechaun, camped out under a billboard, she gets drawn into a century-old crime involving a real pot of gold. Interpol agent Cameron O'Dea is trying to solve the crime. In the process, he takes over the homeless shelter that Julia runs, camps out in her neighbor's RV, and generally turns her life upside down!

Kingdom Come, Amanda MacLean
ISBN 1-57673-120-0
In 1902, feisty Ivy Rose Clayborne, M.D., returns to her hometown of Kingdom Come to fight the coal mining company that is ravaging the land. She meets an unexpected ally, a man who claims to be a drifter but in reality is Harrison MacKenzie, grandson of the coal mining baron. Together they face the aftermath of betrayal, the fight for justice…and the price of love.

A Mother's Love, Bergren, Colson, MacLean
ISBN 1-57673-106-5
Three popular Palisades authors bring you heartwarming stories about the joys and challenges of romance in the midst of motherhood.
By Lisa Bergren: A widower and his young daughter go to Southern California for vacation, and return with much more than they expected.
By Constance Colson: Cassie Jenson wants her old sweetheart to stay in her memories. But when he moves back to town, they find out that they could never forget each other.
By Amanda MacLean: A couple is expecting their first baby, and they hardly have enough time for each other. With the help of an old journal and a last-minute getaway, they work to rekindle their love.

❧

Also look for our new line:

PALISADES PREMIER
More Story. More Romance.

Arabian Winds, Linda Chaikin
ISBN 1-57673-105-7
In the first book of the Lions of the Desert trilogy, World War I is breaking upon the deserts of Arabia in 1914. Young nurse Allison Wescott is on holiday with an archaeological club, but a murder interrupts her plans, and a mysterious officer keeps turning up wherever she goes!
Watch for more books in Linda Chaikin's Egypt series!

Song of the Highlands, Sharon Gillenwater
ISBN 0-88070-946-4
During the Napoleonic Wars, Kiernan is a piper, but he comes back to find out he's inherited a title. At his run-down estate, he meets the beautiful Mariah. During a trip to London, they face a kidnapping...and discover their love for each other.
Watch for more books in Sharon Gillenwater's Scottish series!